CO 1 54 79865

MURTON
12/96
-1. APR. 1997
-7. JUL 1997
SEAHAM
17. JUN 1998
22. JUN 1998
29. JUN 1998
28. AUG. 1998

-5. AUG 1999
BELMONT

14. SEP. 2000
17. OCT. 2000
11. DEC 2000
-3. FEB 2001
11. MAY 2001
BRANDON
13. JUN 2001

-6. AUG 2001
30. AUG. 2001
TRAILER 1

IC
21 MAY 2002
DC
28. DEC 2002
CHILTON
01/03
28 APR 2003
19. MAY 2003
-1. AUG 2003
COUNTY HALL
6/05

5479865   B BEA

 **DURHAM COUNTY COUNCIL**
Arts, Libraries and Museums Department

Please return or renew this item by the last date shown.
Fines will be charged if the book is kept after this date.
Thank you for using *your* library.

 100% recycled paper

A Disgraceful Affair

Women's Life Writings from Around the World
Edited by Marilyn Yalom

Also available in the series

Efronia: An Armenian Love Story
STINA KATCHADOURIAN

Sketches from My Past: Encounters with India's Oppressed
MAHADEVI VARMA

Auschwitz: A Doctor's Story
LUCIE ADELSBERGER

BIANCA LAMBLIN

A Disgraceful Affair

Simone de Beauvoir,

Jean-Paul Sartre,
&
Bianca Lamblin

Translated by Julie Plovnick

NORTHEASTERN UNIVERSITY PRESS
BOSTON

Northeastern University Press

Originally published in France as *Mémoires d'une jeune fille dérangée*; copyright 1993 by Éditions Balland

Translation copyright 1996 by Julie Plovnick

All rights reserved. Except for the quotation of short passages for the purposes of criticism and review, no part of this book may be reproduced in any form or by any means, electronic or mechanical, including photocopying, recording, or any information storage and retrieval system now known or to be invented, without written permission of the publisher.

Library of Congress Cataloging-in-Publication Data
Lamblin, Bianca, 1921–
[Mémoires d'une jeune fille dérangée. English]
A Disgraceful Affair : Simone de Beauvoir, Jean-Paul Sartre, and Bianca Lamblin / Bianca Lamblin ; translated by Julie Plovnick.
p. cm. — (Women's life writings from around the world)
ISBN 1-55553-251-9 (cloth : alk. paper)
1. Beauvoir, Simone de, 1908–   —Friends and associates.
2. Sartre, Jean Paul, 1905–   —Friends and associates.
3. Lamblin, Bianca, 1921–   —Friends and associates.
4. Authors, French—20th
century—Biography. I. Title. II. Series.
PQ2603.E362Z76513   1996
848'.91409—dc20   95-38308

Designed by Diane Levy

Composed in Goudy by Coghill Composition, Richmond, Virginia. Printed and bound by Thomson-Shore, Inc., Dexter, Michigan. The paper is Glatfelter Supple Opaque Recycled, an acid-free stock.

MANUFACTURED IN THE UNITED STATES OF AMERICA
00   99   98   97   96   5   4   3   2   1

To Marianne and Sylvia

Contents

Foreword ix

Introduction 3

CHAPTER ONE
The Threesome 15

CHAPTER TWO
The War 53

CHAPTER THREE
The Postwar Years 129

Notes 175

Foreword

Jean-Paul Sartre and Simone de Beauvoir were a uniquely influential couple. Writers, philosophers, teachers, political activists, and sacred cows, they colored the thinking of two generations of postwar intellectuals. Having rejected the rival ideologies of Freudianism and surrealism, they offered their own brand of existentialism as a way of life.

I was one of those 1950s college students who returned from France smitten by the high priest and high priestess of existentialism. I was determined to spread their humanistic gospel to the unenlightened: God was conclusively dead, we were the sole creators of ourselves, only lucidity and commitment could save us. We spoke what purported to be the language of philosophy—of being and nothingness, of existence preceding essence, of authenticity and inauthenticity.

We admired that mature couple who had chosen not to marry and not to have children so as to avoid hypocrisy, biological entrapment, and, worst of all, boredom. And even if we were not daring enough to emulate their model, we secretly envied what they called their "essential" relationship with one another, which did not preclude "contingent" relationships on the side. De Beauvoir and Sartre had flown in the face of societal conventions and soared above them. Or so it seemed. We never asked, for example, what became of the third parties in their "contingent" affairs.

Bianca Lamblin's *Mémoires d'une jeune fille dérangée* (the title is an adaptation of Simone de Beauvoir's *Mémoires d'une jeune fille rangée*) tells us what it was like to be one of those third parties. Seduced both intellectually and sexually by her lycée professor, Mlle de Beauvoir, Bianca was seventeen and de Beauvoir thirty in 1938 when their personal relationship began. The following year, Bianca was passed on to de Beauvoir's "essential" partner, Jean-Paul Sartre, who was thirty-three at the time.

For a short period, the two professors and the lycée student constituted a threesome. Then, in 1940, at the outbreak of World War II, Bianca found herself abandoned by her dual mentors and lovers. The fact that Bianca Lamblin, née Bienenfeld, was Jewish and likely to be deported by the Nazis did not seem to have given either Sartre or de Beauvoir pause. They had their own troubles in 1940, as did the rest of the French.

When in 1945 Lamblin and de Beauvoir rekindled the friendship that was to last until the older woman's death forty years later, the younger woman tried to forget how shabbily she had been treated. Married during the war years to one of Sartre's former lycée students, Bianca found in her husband, Bernard, a deep source of love and support. Theirs was a more traditional union with children, regular employment as teachers, and the absence of "contingent" relationships.

Bianca had learned the hard way that what sounds good as an abstraction does not always work in real life. She had been a third party in a triangle that, when broken, almost broke her. Her periodic bouts of severe depression that began in 1941 were, according to her retrospective interpretation, linked not only to the Nazi horrors but also to the sense of betrayal she had experienced at the hands of de Beauvoir and Sartre. And this sense of betrayal was reactivated in 1990 when Lamblin read the posthumously published versions of de Beauvoir's war years' journal and letters to Sartre—works that referred directly to Bianca in a tone of ridicule and contempt. Then, without Bernard at her side (he had died in 1978), without the looming figures of Sartre and de Beauvoir (they had died in 1980 and 1986 respectively), Bianca exploded with her own story.

The reader who believes at the onset that this literary outburst was only an act of retaliation will be pleasantly surprised. Her story is much more than a delayed reaction motivated by a desire for revenge. Like most good autobiography, Lamblin's memoir seeks to understand those primary influences that shape a life—in her case, the long-term influence of de Beauvoir and Sartre.

That Bianca Bienenfeld Lamblin survived their rude treatment and the brutal war years, during which she lost close relatives and barely escaped with her own life, was the result of certain mysterious inner strengths that we call courage and endurance. Her survival was also due, in part, to the commitment of her husband, who is in many ways the hero of this story. Bernard Lamblin loved the young

Bianca at a time when female sexual adventures were considered scandalous. He took her as a wife when it was dangerous for a French Catholic to marry a Jewish woman of Polish origins. He sustained her throughout her long bouts of depression, which were gradually brought under control by medication. Lamblin seems to have truly understood the meaning of commitment. What we would give to have his story as well!

Bianca Lamblin offers a compelling narrative of several dramatic episodes in her adult years—her participation in the wartime resistance and her political activities during the war in Algeria, for example. But most of all, it is her friendship with Simone de Beauvoir that occupies center stage and forces us to contemplate a side of that great woman we would prefer to ignore. In the end, we are forced to add another unflattering picture to the de Beauvoir/Sartre album. That is not to say that we should burn the idols of our youth. Like all human idols, de Beauvoir and Sartre were humanly fallible. Clearly their treatment of Bianca Lamblin was not their finest hour. It is to de Beauvoir's credit that she took responsibility for Lamblin's deteriorating mental condition in 1945 when she wrote to Sartre: "I think it is our fault. . . . She is the only person we have really harmed."

Marilyn Yalom
Institute for Research on Women and Gender
Stanford University
June 1995

A Disgraceful Affair

Introduction

*F*inally, after much hesitation, I have decided to recount what was a dramatic episode in my life. Actually, I am forced by outside events to write this story, however reluctantly. If my story is out of the ordinary, it is probably because two of the main characters are Simone de Beauvoir and Jean-Paul Sartre. Together we formed a threesome, or at least that is what I was led to believe.

Now that the summer of 1990 has passed, I shall attempt to relate that dramatic time as I experienced it, to bear witness, to come out from behind a pseudonym, and finally to speak with my own voice to my contemporaries. I am perfectly aware that some people may ridicule my story—speaking out against such eminent figures as Simone de Beauvoir and Sartre will seem quite presumptuous to those who still admire them. I am taking that risk. The way that Simone de Beauvoir and then Sartre treated me in 1940, the humiliation and suffering they caused me, were so severe that the simple truth I want to tell will, I hope, ring truer and clearer than the lies in *Letters to Sartre*. The sorrow I felt in 1940 was reawakened fifty years later, when I read *Letters* and *Journal de guerre*,[1] published at the same time. The meaning of what I had experienced earlier, but had not understood at the time, was finally revealed to me.

I tried many times to write about this experience. In vain. Something always held me back; I was blocked by a powerful and unknown obstacle. I could not tell anyone about what had happened to me. I kept it secret from everyone except my husband and, later, my daughters, when they were grown. A few rare friends and classmates at the Sorbonne also surely suspected that I was involved with Simone de Beauvoir and Sartre, but not many.

At the beginning of 1990 Gallimard published *Lettres à Sartre* and *Journal de guerre*, which Simone de Beauvoir had kept from 1939 to 1941. Sylvie le Bon[2] thought it was necessary to publish these writings, which are essentially personal but involve many people and, in particular, the period when my life was turned upside down by meeting Simone de Beauvoir. Sylvie le Bon simply avoided mentioning my name, replacing it with the pseudonym "Louise Védrine."[3] Indeed, some time before this, after reading a blurb in *Le monde* stating that Sylvie le Bon had decided to donate a certain number of Simone de Beauvoir's letters to the Bibliothèque Nationale, I wrote to remind her of Simone de Beauvoir's solemn oath never to mention my name in her letters or memoirs. When I wrote to Ms. le Bon, I had no idea she was preparing *Letters to Sartre* for publication.

However deeply the contents of *Letters* and *Journal de guerre* hurt me, I want to begin my story by saying that I am driven not by a need for revenge but by a simple desire to tell the truth.

The publication of these writings stimulated many articles, some expressing praise, others disgust. I read some of them, which ranged from *Le monde* and *La libération* to *Elle*. Friends had warned me ahead of time, doing their best to dissuade me from reading them. But I am not one to flee from danger. I confront it, even if it is painful. Nevertheless, after buying those three publications I waited several weeks before I dared open them. I was torn by two conflicting emotions: I wanted to know what Simone de Beauvoir had written about me to Sartre, but I was also afraid of knowing. I must admit, some of the excerpts quoted in the press gave me goose bumps!

To convey how deeply I was hurt, I must emphasize that it was not just a matter of distant events that had taken place in my youth; Simone de Beauvoir had remained my friend. Throughout her life, we continued to see each other on a regular basis. I trusted her completely. I thought she could understand everything, and I considered her innately honest. I thought her friendship was sincere, although it was entirely different from the emotional relationship we had had in my youth. She did nothing to destroy my image of her—quite the contrary, she protected it from becoming tainted in any way. Now that I have read *Letters* and *Journal de guerre*, I cannot fathom how I could have been so deeply deceived. While I have always found it difficult to imagine the duplicity of other people, my naïveté does have its limits. In this case, it is as if the idealized image of my teacher that I formed when I was a teenager remained intact my whole life and formed a screen, masking her true feelings. Because Simone de Beauvoir told me very little about herself at that time in the far-off past, and very little about the people close to her, responding with an evasive "There's nothing interesting to say about that" or simply lying; because she carefully avoided having me meet her friends and enter into her world, I did not have much to go on.

I realize now that I was a victim of Sartre's womanizing and of the ambivalent and dubious way the Beaver[4] defended his behavior. I had entered a world of complex relationships that led to pitiful imbroglios, pathetic plotting, and constant lying in which Simone de Beauvoir and Sartre cautiously avoided getting caught. I discovered that Simone de Beauvoir would select ripe young flesh from among her female students and have a taste herself before palming them off, or should I say more vulgarly, thrusting them upon Sartre. In any case, such is the pattern that can explain Olga Kosakievicz's story,[5] as well as my own. Their perversity was carefully concealed beneath Sartre's meek and mild exterior and the Beaver's serious and austere appearance. In fact, they were acting out a commonplace version of *Dangerous Liaisons*.

As for me, I was fully convinced that nothing could come between them. Of course, this belief was based on how Simone de Beauvoir described their feelings and commitment to each other and also corresponded to my own views on love and loyalty. At the time of the "threesome" (that is, in 1939), I was convinced that they both loved me sincerely. The fact that my relationship with each of them was based on their solid, mutual love for each other did not make me jealous in the least; on the contrary, I found this very reassuring. I felt as though I was part of a permanent love triangle. Before I met Sartre, Simone de Beauvoir and I shared only a passionate friendship. As soon as he entered the emotional picture, everything became much more difficult and much more complicated.

The world in which each of them moved was far removed from my own. It was like nothing I had ever known. I was thus at their mercy, knowing nothing of their motives. I was so excited by this double passion, so smitten by the strangeness of our adventure, that I lived, like Madame Bovary, in a sort of dream world that blinded me to their lies and kept me from seeing through the illusions that held me in thrall. It is probably also true that when they embarked on this affair, they were not aware of the fierce emotions deep inside me, or of the high expectations I had about love. To them, our story was mundane, at most a pale version of their threesome with Olga. To me, it was unique, vital; I was totally committed. This is the source of the Beaver's constant complaints in her letters to Sartre about what she called my "pathetic nature," which so often bothered her. But when you play with fire, you never know how far it will spread, how far the wind will carry it.

The other reason—probably less important but nevertheless part of my decision to write my own story—is that I could no longer stand to be a passive object described with relish by biographers and lampoonists. I wanted, finally, to be a *subject* who relates her own experience and no longer a mere *object* for other people.

When Deirdre Bair's biography *Simone de Beauvoir*[6] was published in New York in 1990, I was infuriated. In an apparently well-documented book, Deirdre Bair, an American scholar who prides herself on numerous long interviews with Simone de Beauvoir, tells her version of my story with the two authors. In the text of the biography and in the index of that large book, she gives my maiden name and my married name, and reveals the secret of my pseudonym, Louise Védrine.

When I learned from American relatives that I had thus acquired a certain dubious fame, I was alarmed and outraged, since my usual line of action had been to keep quiet about the story of the "threesome," and I had asked Simone de Beauvoir and Sartre never to mention my name in their works (and they had promised not to). Since I did not know many people in the United States, and American law does not protect private life, it was futile and impossible to attack the book, which had already been published and was selling well. But I was very worried about a probable translation into French. Here in France, both my husband and I know a great number of people. Bernard had many students, and I have had several generations of my own, not to mention all our friends and colleagues. Although Deirdre Bair's book does contain known facts, it also includes numerous questionable claims bordering on libel.

I therefore consulted a lawyer, who advised me against taking any action in the United States but told me I could warn the future publisher of the French translation that I firmly opposed having my name published and the origin of my pseudonym revealed. Eighteen months of complicated arbitration transpired among Éditions Fayard, Deirdre Bair, and my lawyer. Finally, Ms. Bair agreed to replace my name with her own initials, D.B. In 1991 Fayard published *Simone de Beauvoir* in French.

It is hard to understand Deirdre Bair's way of working. She appears to have accepted at face value—and without ever verifying them—Simone de Beauvoir's cruel and untruthful allegations about me. In addition, Simone de Beauvoir had been very careful never to tell me clearly that an American scholar was preparing an important work about her. The little she did leak out was evasive, often critical, and she "forbade" me to read the book when it was published. This should have raised my suspicions. In her own way, the Beaver had shown her naïveté, but I never paid attention: so much had been written about her by so many people that I was overwhelmed by her fame. I had long ago given up reading everything that was written about her.

Moreover, Simone de Beauvoir had arranged things such that Deirdre Bair would not come into contact with me; she herself would thus remain the only source of information on our shared past. All of this led to a completely unacceptable portrayal of Bernard and me that really shocked me.

Various works[7] published between 1989 and 1991 in which I was mentioned by name thus led me to write my own story about the experience that began when I was almost eighteen years old.

The year 1990, four years after Simone de Beauvoir's death, was pivotal. I had another breakdown, as I had in 1940, fifty years earlier. This time I did not feel crushed by abandonment and heartbreak but deeply saddened, so intensely disappointed that I was nauseated and disgusted when I discovered the true personality of the woman I had loved all my life. A liberating anger rose up inside me, pulled me out of my stupor, and dissolved my shyness and everything that had always restrained me. I was finally free to tell my story.

I shall now give a brief autobiographical account to help the reader understand my background and later evaluate some of Sartre and de Beauvoir's reactions.

I was born in Lublin, Poland, in April 1921 to Jewish parents. When I was fifteen months old, my parents left Poland for Paris, without hoping or wishing to return. An uncle, Jacques Bienenfeld, a successful businessman, wanted to expand his trade in natural pearls from the Orient. He invited several of his Polish and Austrian relatives, all Bienenfelds like himself, to join him in France and work for him in the company he had established there. My father had just completed medical school in Vienna; he hesitated greatly before giving up a medical career, even though he was aware that such a career would be very difficult for a Jew. Finally, he accepted my uncle's offer and the possibility of a completely new life.

It was a difficult decision, but my father always held firm once he had made up his mind. In addition, in 1920 my mother was also expecting my birth, another reason to emigrate. The insecurity of central Europe and particularly of Poland, periodically hit by violent anti-Semitic movements, led Jews to flee to more democratic lands. Hence, my father's loss of career was offset by the hope of a free and happier life in a country where he could raise his children in a peaceful environment. We thus became French citizens, and I have always considered myself French.

When they arrived in Paris in 1922, my parents were very poor. At first they lived in two small rooms on the seventh floor of a building without an elevator with my father's brother, my aunt, and my little cousin, Nicha, who was my age. Since none of them spoke French, they could not hope to find work before learning the language; they studied hard and progressed rapidly in their courses at Berlitz.

Our financial situation gradually improved, and my parents were able to move to a real apartment. Unfortunately, a little later, when I was about six years old, my mother contracted pleurisy. That was in 1927, just before my sister, Ela, was born. The doctors sent my mother to a health resort; my newborn sister and I were left in the hands of nannies. My father had to travel often, since he was in charge of buying natural pearls in the place where they were cultivated: the island of Bahrain, in the Persian Gulf. The family was scattered. It was thus decided that my sister and I should move closer to Mother: we spent nearly two years in a small hotel in the town of Leysin. Twice a week our nanny took us to see Mother in her sanatorium higher up in the mountains. This childhood separation deeply marked me and especially my little sister. The shock I felt during my mother's illness, when I learned that she might die, affected my health. Photos from that time show a skinny, shy, nervous little girl with huge dark circles under her eyes. Every night I threw up my dinner. The so-called friends I made at the hotel often ganged up on me. They knew my sadness made me weak, and they would pick on me. During the winter my sister and I were kept almost naked, as prescribed by a doctor whose name I have forgotten; that was how we first learned to ski. The sun was supposed to prevent all illnesses. So living in Switzerland and not going to school was not all bad.

When we returned to France, my uncle wanted to have my father close at hand (he saw more and more that he could count on him). My parents rented a villa with a big garden, right next to my uncle's luxurious residence on Rue des Bons-Raisins in Suresnes. My parents' democratic convictions led them to enroll me at the École Communale du Plateau, in the middle of a working-class housing development, where I was able to catch up after all my years out of school. I was a lively, intelligent, absent-minded child, curious about everything, skinny and anemic. My head was covered with dark copper-colored curls. My mother, who was a good seamstress, made me beautiful dresses. She infused in me her sense of style. But the school I went to, the setting in which I spent my days, did not accept such finery. I remember the day I arrived in the schoolyard wearing a beret perched on the side of my head the way my mother had arranged it. I was greeted by a general outcry: the usual way to wear a beret was right on top of the head, pulled down almost to the eyes. Cruelly mocking me, my classmates seized my beret and threw it from one person to the next. Meanwhile, frantic and crying, I ran all over the place trying to get it back. At nine years old, I obviously could not appreciate the beauty of the class struggle! Even though at that time I was lucky enough to have my mother back, and our family life was more normal, I still have mixed feelings about those two years in Suresnes: unhappy at school, happy in my own garden.

I got into the habit of climbing up to the fork of a tall cedar tree to spend the afternoon reading a book. I read a lot, and since I was a fast reader and my parents could not constantly supply me with new books, I would reread the same, often inane books over and over again. I went through the entire Bibliothèque Rose series,[8] starting with books by the Comtesse de Ségur. I also delighted in the touching caricature of *Ces dames aux chapeaux verts* by Acremant, and I discovered unknown horizons with *White Fang*. Later I savored *Little Fadette* and other charming books by George Sand, then various works by Anatole France and Alphonse Daudet. I also liked comic strips, such as "Bécassine," "Les pieds nickelés," and "Les aventures de Bicot."

When I was ten, I had to think about going to a lycée. My parents decided to move back to Paris to make it more convenient for me to go to school there. They rented a small apartment in the Sixteenth Arrondissement, and in October I entered Lycée Molière. I was a good student and a hard worker, interested in many different subjects. I was especially proud of being the best in Latin. Besides the lycée, I began going to the International Conservatory of Music, and I practiced the piano much more than I had in Suresnes. My parents bought a Pleyel grand piano. I loved the pure sound it produced. My mother pushed me to do music out of personal regret: despite her true artistic sense, she had never had access to any form of art while growing up in a very poor Polish family. She projected onto me her frustrated desire.

Before long, I made great progress, and at the end of the seventh grade Pierre Lucas, the director of the conservatory, called in my mother to tell her to take me out of the lycée. He wanted me to devote five or six hours each day to the piano, because he thought I was particularly talented and could pursue a career as a pianist. My parents were very reluctant, but the piano was my passion, and I had firmly and willingly decided to devote myself to my instrument. I fought the entire summer. I screamed and cried. I was so sure of myself and so persistent that I was able to convince my parents to give in. At the start of the next school year, I took private lessons in general studies and worked on my piano the rest of the time. This arrangement lasted two years. At the end of this period, after deep reflection and consideration of my weaknesses and the pitfalls of an artist's career, I gave up the idea of becoming a concert pianist and decided to return to my studies. So I returned to the lycée and confronted all the difficulties caused by my two-year absence. Missing the eighth and ninth grades left me sorely lacking. But with hard work, I graduated on time.

The nature of my reading had changed a bit. I liked the sickly sweet stories of Frédéric Delly but also followed my teachers' advice and took up real literature. My mother's best friend, a very cultured woman, gave me a beautifully bound edition of Joseph Bédier's version of *Tristan and Isolde*. I was so fascinated by that legend, so taken by its style and the superb adventure it recounts, that I read the book over and over again. Much later, I learned from Denis de Rougemont's study *Love in the Western World* that not only all of literature but even people's views in the West were influenced by this legendary model. I think it was at once informative and influential for me: I liked it because it was a beautiful and tragic love story, but it probably fostered my tendency to be sentimental.

ONE

The Threesome

My life changed forever when Simone de Beauvoir, newly appointed to Lycée Molière, walked into my classroom. It was the start of the 1937 academic year. We were all thrilled at the idea of having a beautiful young woman as a teacher, instead of the boring old man who did duty in the class next door. I have no clear memory of the first time I saw her. Instead, I have a general impression: she was petite, slender, a bit clumsy, not very well built. She walked quickly and sometimes made abrupt gestures. She was all energy and no calm; she must have been somewhat nervous, because she kept scratching a big bump on her left hand, sometimes until it bled. What made the deepest impression on me was the beauty of her sculpted, perfectly proportioned face, with its classic profile and pronounced cheekbones. The intelligence in her luminous blue eyes struck us right from the start. Her only flaw was her broken, hoarse, rather unpleasant voice. Her extremely rapid speech made it difficult for us to take notes. Sometimes she spoke so fast that a bold student like me would beg, "Please speak more slowly, Mademoiselle!" She would slow down, but only for a second: in the heat of the lecture, she would soon race back to breakneck speed.

I was fascinated as much by the teacher as by the philosophical topics she introduced in her lectures. The whole package came as a revelation to me. She knew so much about subjects that were so rich and so new to us; her lectures were lively, clear, and well structured; she never used any notes; she had everything stored in her mind, in perfect order. She expressed approval as easily as disdain. Had I been older, I might have found her forwardness tiresome, even suspicious, but a sixteen-year-old is easily impressed. Simone de Beauvoir always had a way of passing peremptory judgments. One day forty years later, when I expressed admiration for Yves Nat's sober and profound interpretation of Beethoven's sonatas, she cut me off: "Not at all, Wilhelm Kempff plays them best." Her tone was so final that there was no room for disagreement. I gave up, once again, on any sort of discussion. No matter what, the Beaver was always right.

Simone de Beauvoir's light brown, rather thin hair was arranged in two smooth, symmetric coils atop her well-proportioned head. A thin braid ran from one ear to the other. I remember the checkered skirts and tight-fitting suits she wore. Later, when I knew her better, she told me her mother made her clothes to save money. When we had become even closer, I noticed that the little white collars peeking over the lapels of her suits were not shirt collars but false shirt fronts held in place by an elastic band around the chest. Since I took pride in my sense of style, I laughed at this pathetic little trick, especially since I discovered on the same occasion that the braid was also fake. During the war Simone learned, thanks to her hairstylist, that she could make an elegant crown with a sort of bun on top of her coils. You can see this hairstyle in certain old photos. Later on, she adopted the famous colorful turban hairstyle. She was very proud of her invention and often mentions it in the letters she wrote to Sartre when he was a soldier. I thought she was above such coquettish behavior. I was wrong.

Besides her obvious beauty, what was most striking about her was her brilliant, piercing, bold intelligence. The power and speed of her comprehension was startling, her thirst to read unquenchable. In everyday life, she never wasted time and was always in a hurry, something I could not understand. Much later, I asked her to explain her constant sense of urgency. "Life is so short," she sighed, revealing the connection between her obsessive fear of death and her habit of running words together and cramming her days full of meetings. She lived every experience, however powerful, in depth, filing it away in her very precise memory and rarely repeating anything. One day I invited her to a concert featuring a series of Beethoven quartets. Much to my surprise, she refused, claiming she had already listened to them very carefully and saw no need to do so again. I was shocked to find my friend so excessively intellectual—and so different from me.

In class, her lessons on consciousness focused primarily on Descartes, then on Husserl. When Simone de Beauvoir was explaining the Cartesian concept of methodical doubt, she paused before getting to the main point and asked,

"Now, then, after you've put everything into doubt, that is, rejected everything, what happens? What's left?" Suddenly inspired, no doubt thanks to my eager attentiveness, I answered, "What is left is that I think." The Cartesian *cogito* had seized hold of me. Yet I have no clear memory of anything related to the unconscious, a concept neither Simone de Beauvoir nor Sartre ever accepted. Simone de Beauvoir probably mentioned Freud to us, but only to tear him apart. According to her, the unconscious could be only an opaque entity *inside* the conscience, that is, something that was impossible. Philosophically, one had to choose either Husserl or Freud. Simone de Beauvoir thus denied the very notion of the unconscious.

On the whole, we had very traditional lessons on the various topics in the course, although things were inevitably slowed down by the amount of time she devoted to the philosophy of science. Because of this, she had to rush through several notions of morality. She explained to us Epicurean philosophy, Stoic logic, and Kantian "morality." During the first term, however, probably feeling she had plenty of time, she lingered on the question of emotions (Sartre later wrote a noteworthy short work entitled *Sketch for a Theory of the Emotions*).[1] She asked students to describe an emotional experience they had had. I raised my hand and recounted an experience I'd had the preceding summer, when my parents were gone and there were no other adults around. A girlfriend and I had to sleep alone in an isolated house in Cabourg. During the evening and at night we were bothered by a strange man who tried to break into the villa. We had no neighbors, no telephone. My friend, terrified, buried her head under a pillow. My heart racing, I mustered up my courage, went to the window, and threatened him with the wrath of my father, who I claimed was about to return. Miraculously, the man left. Later, Simone de Beauvoir told me that she first noticed me that day in class and was charmed by the way I told my story.

She had regard for the brilliant students, the elite capable of taking an interest in philosophical discussions. She felt biting disdain toward the others. This disdain was evident in the way she commented on poor work. She was so harsh that I felt sorry for my classmates. Later, I communicated my disapproval, but she would have none of it. All that mattered to her was intelligence. Since she thought I was intelligent enough and thought I was the best student in the class, I had a right to her attention.

Around March 1938 (when I was almost seventeen), I wrote her a short letter expressing my interest in philosophy and my admiration for her. I remember how touched I was when, very shortly thereafter, I received a reply by express delivery inviting me to meet her at the Brasserie Lumina on Rue de Rennes, near where her mother lived. She greeted me warmly; we decided to start seeing each other outside of class that very year, so that we might get to know each other better. I was at once intimidated, thrilled, and proud to have earned the right to see her privately. I was floating on a cloud of happiness.

I was especially entranced by her physical presence, but this very presence reflected her determined, unyielding nature. She was like a ship's prow speeding through the waves, a prow made of a solid, brilliant, unchangeable stone. I thought she had neither weaknesses (I was wrong) nor complexity (wrong again). She was a "force in motion," traveling full speed ahead without faltering, sacrificing everything for fame and perhaps glory. Touched by my passionate declaration of friendship, she was tender and caring toward me. This blinded me to her ferocious egoism and even her voracious ambition.

I was also entranced by the disparity between her knowledge, which seemed vast, and my own, which was rather meager at the time. It was meager because my immigrant parents had no deep knowledge of French literature in its entirety. They liked only certain classic nineteenth- and twentieth-century authors. Every year, my mother modestly asked my French teacher for advice on what I should read. The combination of all these elements is probably what made me feel that I was in the presence of someone who dominated me in all respects.

Because it was difficult for us to meet during the week, we met almost every Sunday that spring, to stroll around Paris or the surrounding areas. Waking up Sunday morning was a joy for me. I would run to catch the Metro at Passy station, near my family's house. The train would emerge from the bowels of the earth; I would jump into one of the cars and be thrust upward, between the hills of Meudon and the Eiffel Tower. I was so terribly impatient for the end of my ride; I don't think I have ever felt so strongly about any other ride in my entire life. We passed countless stations. The time en route felt like an enemy standing between me and what I desired. Finally, I would get out at Edgar-Quinet and run all the way down Rue de la Gaîté into the rather seedy-looking Hôtel Mistral on Rue Cels, a tiny street near

Rue Froidevaux, where she lived. We would greet each other warmly, then decide on the plan for the day: we would go around Paris, visiting areas I never knew existed. We would wander around the flea market or stroll through Montmartre. Sometimes we would take a train to the suburbs, as we did the day we took a long walk on the terrace of Saint-Germain. Once I suggested we visit the street in Suresnes where I had lived and stop at the "château," which had been Uncle Jacques's home.

Uncle Jacques was the heart of the family, the anchoring force that determined our fate. Had he not invited us to join him in Paris, my father would have remained a lowly Jewish doctor in Poland; then, with the rise of Nazism, we would probably have all been killed. Uncle Jacques was like a character in a legend, loved and feared at the same time. He possessed true powers of creation, having "made" himself in the manner of the American self-made man. He probably arrived in Paris, penniless, before the First World War. No one knows how he was able to become the world's leading Oriental pearl merchant in just a few years. His genius reached far beyond business. He was friendly with Henri Sellier, the socialist mayor of Suresnes. Because he had consulted the Institut Pasteur about the structure of pearls and their flaws, he maintained warm relations with Professor Calmette.[2] He commissioned his personal cabinetmaker, whose home and workshop were located on the château grounds, to reconstruct church pews in the château's entry hall, which was adorned with two enormous statues—copies of Michelangelo's *Slaves*, from the Louvre. Three gardeners bustled about the park and vegetable garden. From the tennis courts echoed the cries of young people playing. Jacques was a true dictator, reigning over both his luxurious domain and the staff in his office on Rue Fayette. He was generous toward those he loved, odious toward others. Like many other businessmen who had achieved fleeting success, he was suddenly and completely ruined by the 1929 stock market crash. He owed the banks so much money that they confiscated all his merchandise. There was nothing he could do. Demoralized and ill, he died not many years later.

We reached the highlands of Suresnes beneath Mount Valérien. My uncle had been dead for a long time, and his house was abandoned. The superb yet melancholy park lay waste, ravaged and pillaged. The "château" was wide open, empty. Heavyhearted, I was deeply moved to have returned to one of the places of my childhood. We went up to the second floor. We sat there in the sun, right on the floor of the balcony of Aunt Germaine's bedroom. We talked for a long time: I talked about my past, and Simone described the main events of her own. I told her about where I came from, how I had bounced around from place to place during my childhood. I described the members of my family and explained my decision to become a pianist, followed by my change of mind. She, in turn, talked about her friendship with Zaza, whom she had met at the Cours Désir, an exclusive private school, when she was only eleven. In *Memoirs of a Dutiful Daughter*,[3] published in 1958, Simone describes each phase of her long and loyal attachment to Elisabeth Le Coin, whom she calls "Zaza" in her book: "But in Zaza I could glimpse a presence, flashing as a spring of water, solid as a block of marble, and as firmly drawn as a portrait by Dürer." Zaza's talents and grace made Simone de Beauvoir feel almost inferior. She told me of Zaza's sudden death from encephalitis at the age of twenty-one. Zaza's death left Simone de Beauvoir with a deep, persistent sadness.[4] Then Simone told me how she had fought the prejudices of her milieu to obtain the right to pursue advanced studies. Finally, she described how she had met a group of students at the École Normale Supérieure: Herbaud, Sartre, and Nizan. To end this story, as if with a deftly prepared finale, she said, "The one who was the ugliest, the filthiest, but also the nicest and most supremely intelligent was Sartre." And I knew immediately that he was the love of her life.

She revealed to me the type of relationship they had: no marriage—above all, no marriage. No children—they're too demanding. Free to live their own lives and have their own sentimental and sexual adventures. Their only promise was to tell each other everything, never to lie. In sum, absolute freedom with complete openness. An ambitious goal! Most of all, they wanted lives full of travel, encounters, studies, and the exchange of ideas with intelligent people; lives in which they could show what they were made of and perhaps achieve a degree of fame that would allow them to transmit a new way of thinking to future generations.

I tried to understand the reasons for these choices but could not, since I knew nothing of Simone de Beauvoir's and Sartre's emotional life. Simone had told me about Olga Kosakievicz, explaining that their friendship had cooled quite a bit and that she no longer saw Olga unless she had to. I also learned that Olga's sister, Wanda, was Sartre's lover. I was repulsed by what I heard about the casual, capricious, lazy, and irresponsible lifestyle of the two sisters. I could not conceive of how they got by solely on the generosity of Sartre and Simone de Beauvoir, who often had a rather difficult time making ends meet. The reasons Sartre and Simone de Beauvoir accepted this situation were complex, having to do with spontaneous generosity and the determined rejection of strictly "bourgeois" financial prudence. I think the main reason, however, was their fascination with a lifestyle more improvident than their own, which compensated for their boredom as civil servants. Their generosity might also have stemmed from feelings of guilt for earning a regular income, rather than living the bohemian life.

Their day-to-day existence brought them into contact with many different people; this made for a disjointed schedule, a series of meetings that precluded any sort of flexibility or spontaneity in their friendships. Simone de Beauvoir organized her time extremely strictly, like a patch-

Simone de Beauvoir, wearing a plaid blouse, sits in the front row of this 1938 class photo at the Lycée Molière in Paris. Seated on her right, wearing a white blouse, is Bianca Bienenfeld.

work quilt. You could measure her affection, as it were, or the level of interest she had in a person by the amount of time allotted to him or her. She would meet people one after another, often at the same café table, but her various friends rarely met. Looking back at this situation, it's easy to see that her own selfishness was like a shield protecting her.

At the beginning of my friendship with Simone de Beauvoir, I knew Sartre only from what she told me; I saw him through her eyes. But I was well aware that I did not know the most important thing, that is, how they influenced each other. Later, after I had met Sartre, I noticed that a likemindedness strengthened their attachment, despite their very different natures. Since their beliefs about everyday life and their philosophical ideas matched, it was difficult to make a thorough analysis of their differences. They seemed to be a stone slab with two faces, a sort of Janus figure.

Nevertheless, from the very first months I identified myself ardently with Simone de Beauvoir. I did everything to get closer to her, to such an extent that my classmates later made fun of the speech habits I had picked up from her. In any case, I was quite different from the little girl who had once answered the banal question, "What do you want to do when you grow up?" with the naïve response, "Get married and have children," which made Simone purse her lips in disapproval and fall silent. Around June, even before graduating from high school, I knew I wanted to get a degree in philosophy and teach, just like her.

But I did not identify with Simone de Beauvoir completely. We were different, first and foremost because I was Jewish. My parents had taught me to be generous, truthful, and loyal; Simone, on the contrary, made it clear that she selfishly did only what pleased her or was to her advantage. Her influence caused me to change some of my ideas, however: for example, I no longer believed that a woman should maintain her chastity or virginity until marriage. I lost my prejudice toward homosexuals. But I still believed in hard work, honesty, and loyalty. I aspired to become financially independent. I was firmly convinced that women could achieve a sense of dignity only by having a job. For me, this idea was far from new; I did not learn it from Simone. I had always known I had to work, both because my family was not very wealthy and because I knew from experience that good luck could change. In addition, these were the beliefs of my father who, in this respect, had raised me as a boy. (Remember, my story takes place during the 1930s, when bourgeois fathers generally dreamed only of marrying off their daughters properly.) Above all, my mother was a counterexample, a negative role model for me: she would have loved to work but had no practical experience and was reduced to asking my father for money each month to support the family. Mama often said, "Become independent; don't put yourself in the position of having to beg for money from a man!" Thus the desire to work was instilled in me from a very early age.

My relationship with Simone de Beauvoir was therefore complex. I found her attractive and fascinating, but I could not fully identify with her. It was as if I had entered a magic castle and left behind some of my ideas—the way you take off your shoes when entering a mosque—but could not get any further than the entry hall. There were, in fact, many more differences between us than I had imagined. This would become evident in time.

The Threesome

Sartre and Simone de Beauvoir had invented a bizarre term to describe their relationship: it was a "morganatic marriage," a very pompous expression used to describe the marriage "between a prince and a woman of inferior rank." The way they described their pact revealed their ambiguity on the subject: they rejected the rite of marriage but felt the need to create a substitute. It was very difficult for me to understand why, when a woman loved a man the way Simone loved Sartre, she would refuse to live with him and not want to have children together. It was obvious that living in a hotel and eating in restaurants saved a lot of time, and I saw that Simone was neither interested in nor inclined toward housework. But with regard to children, I had not yet realized to what extent the very idea of having children deeply disgusted them both. Since I did not yet know Sartre and probably had a completely false idea about his relationship with de Beauvoir, I was not able to understand why they allowed each other total freedom. I could not understand their relationship, because I imagined they fully trusted each other and were never jealous. The Beaver never told me of her worries, of the anxiety she sometimes felt. She maintained the "official" theory of their pact. During her partner's many love affairs, she appeared to remain calm. This calmness contributed to my idealized image of my friend. Much later, various sources I read revealed that the emotional security the Beaver displayed did have its cracks. Several events involving Olga and Wanda, and later Dolorès Vanetti[5] and maybe even my own adventures with Sartre, caused her anguish and distress. But when I was young, in 1938 and 1939, I could never have imagined the unrest in her soul. I was convinced that their mutual commitment was unfailing and clearly defined. That was enough for me.

"Sartre took pleasure in the company of women, finding them less comic than men. He had no intention, at twenty-three, of renouncing their tempting variety. He explained the matter to me in his favorite terminology. 'What *we* have,' he said, 'is an essential love; but it is a good idea for us also to experience *contingent* love affairs,' " wrote Simone de Beauvoir in *The Prime of Life*.[6] Moving beyond the philosophical jargon, it seems that in the first stage of their relationship it was Sartre who, out of an irrepressible urge to pursue women, had imposed this pact on the Beaver. If you think about it, this pact differs in but one important respect from the usual behavior of married men, whether they be bourgeois or working class: the promise to tell each other all about one's "contingent" love affairs.[7] The other thing that made it unique was the mutuality: since the Beaver gave him complete freedom, why would Sartre care whether or not she too was fooling around? On the contrary, this mutuality guaranteed his freedom. Besides, he took advantage of this permission much earlier and much more frequently than she. When I was getting to know them, I believed they had a novel pact that was nonetheless based on mutuality and equality. Much later, I saw it was a "trick" that Sartre had invented to satisfy his need for sexual conquest and that Simone de Beauvoir was forced to accept. Hiding behind the philosophical justification for the pact was a sort of bribery: "Take it or leave it!" And what cannot be won with pretty words? Sartre was unbeatable in this domain. The Beaver was perhaps his main dupe.

The Threesome

Looking back, I suddenly wondered how Simone de Beauvoir described their sex life (she never spoke to me about it). I once again consulted *The Prime of Life*. To my surprise, I found nothing whatsoever. Nothing. When I first read it, I thought this silence—regarding something so important to a couple and essential for an author writing about herself—reflected a certain reserve, a discretion that fit in well with the severity of the memoirs. But the contents of recently published works, including *Letters to Sartre* and *Journal de guerre*, make it difficult not to be shocked by the contrast. Indeed, when someone else's personal life is concerned, Simone de Beauvoir tells all, without the slightest reserve and often with all the shocking details. She even tends to embellish and exaggerate stories, in order to feed the fantasies of the poor, undersexed reader. This explains the inconsistencies, the lies, the detailed descriptions of the supposed lovemaking of the Beaver and her female friends. Her silence can no longer be attributed to delicate reserve; maybe there was just not much to tell. I'm sure that the fairly hot-blooded Beaver was deeply disappointed in her first physical relations with Sartre.

Several years after their mutual pact of 1929, Sartre already preferred to seek out new experiences with other women or girls, instead of with the Beaver. When I knew Simone de Beauvoir, she and Sartre were no longer having sex with each other. One day much later, she herself hinted at her disappointment when, surprisingly, we were talking about the past. I told her that Sartre was a very poor lover; far from contradicting me, as I had expected, she agreed immediately, saying that he was not very skilled in that domain. And our conversation stopped there, as usual, because the past weighed so heavily, and there was so much to tell that it was better to remain silent. But her very agreement revealed a great deal about their relationship.

Simone de Beauvoir first knew truly sensual love with Nelson Algren, her American lover. He gave her a new awareness of herself.[8] The contrast between their relationship and her purely intellectual relationship with Sartre is fascinating. This makes it even more amazing that she decided to leave Algren, who was very much in love with her, in order to remain with Sartre.

Now that I've discussed Sartre and de Beauvoir's ambiguous views on life, I shall continue my own story. Spring passed as follows: work during the week, walks on Sundays. My attachment to the Beaver (whom I still called Simone at the time) became stronger each day and very passionate, while my enthusiasm for philosophy increased. We were very close but not physically involved. When I graduated, she invited me on a short backpacking trip in the Morvan.

I have forgotten our exact itinerary, but I can still feel the humidity that bathed the mountainous, wooded, wild landscape. I was fairly athletic, but I was not used to long hikes. We hiked about twenty kilometers per day, which really wore me out. Simone, on the other hand, was a very tough, seasoned hiker—she urged me forward with a hint of impatience.

One evening we arrived exhausted in a small village with only one inn and asked for a room. The innkeeper began by saying there were not any left, and then, weeping, she told us the cause of her sorrow: her son had left to work far away from her. She cried and cried. Finally, she showed us a plain room with no electricity, sparsely furnished with a double bed and an extremely rusty washbasin and pitcher. When we inquired about the bathroom, she pointed toward the garden. As for dinner, she did not want to give us anything: we bargained endlessly for just an omelet and a piece of bread. It was during this trip that we began, shyly at first, our physical involvement. After five days of hiking, we arrived at Vézelay and stopped for a visit. We stayed at a welcoming and comfortable, charming hotel not far from the Basilique de la Madeleine. After washing up thoroughly, we dressed up in our best clothes and went down to the dining room. Simone complimented me on my pink linen suit. The next day, in the bus back to Paris, we held hands tenderly. This seemed to shock some of the passengers.

The summer split us apart. I went on a trip to Annecy with my family, but I could not wait to begin college and see Simone again. When classes began at the Sorbonne, it was decided I would meet Sartre's three students, who also wanted to major in philosophy. The Beaver gave me Sartre's description of his students from Lycée Pasteur. As for me, I was easy to recognize, thanks to the red highlights in my hair. Our first course was held at Sainte-Anne Hospital, because all of us had chosen psychopathology for our certificate in psychology. In the steeply sloping little amphitheater, we all met eagerly: Jean Kanapa, always brooding and sarcastic; Raoul Lévy, with his flaming red hair; and Bernard Lamblin, with his wild, silent, poetlike presence, who nonetheless became irresistibly silly when he was with

Raoul. Since I was to marry Bernard about three years later, you could say that, in a way, we were Sartre and Simone de Beauvoir's offspring! But this is, of course, just a bad joke, since nothing was further from their minds than the marriage of their disciples, let alone the very idea of marriage.⁹ From that day on, we were never apart. We worked as a tight, efficient team. We were well organized, determined to complete our studies quickly, fascinated by philosophical discussions. We invented group work, rarely practiced at the Sorbonne at the time. We exchanged our lecture notes, gave each other oral reports, took turns going to certain less interesting courses.

A little later that year, three of us submitted an assignment together to Paul Guillaume.¹⁰ Never before had the

Jean-Paul Sartre's philosophy class in the spring of 1938. Sartre sits in the middle of the front row, looking away from the camera. At the top left of the photo stands Bernard Lamblin, Bianca Bienenfeld's future husband.

Sorbonne seen students with such nerve: Bernard and I wrote the paper, since Raoul, by far the most intelligent of the four of us, was overcome with a sort of writer's block whenever he had to make a presentation or write a paper. After rewarding us with a very high grade, Paul Guillaume called us into his office to demand an explanation. We insisted that all three of us had contributed to the preparation and writing of the paper. In the end, he believed us, against his will, but became angry because we supported the arguments in our paper with ideas from his famous book *La psychologie de la forme*. Annoyed, he insisted, "Everyone labels me a gestaltist because I presented the theories of gestalt psychology, but that's not true. I don't believe in it!" We were speechless, having believed this popular illusion ourselves!

Sartre was having a difficult time then, although we had no idea this was the case. Because Sartre was interested in all matters relating to images, one of his former classmates, Dr. Lagache, invited him to Sainte-Anne for an injection of mescaline, a harmless hallucinogenic drug. But to the doctors' surprise, the drug had astonishingly disproportionate effects on Sartre: "The objects he looked at changed their appearance in the most horrifying manner: umbrellas became vultures, shoes turned into skeletons, and faces acquired monstrous characteristics, while behind him, just past the corner of his eye, swarmed crabs and polyps and grimacing Things."[11] No need to point out the literary use of these horrible experiences in works such as *Nausea* and *The Condemned of Altona*. These bizarre hallucinations persisted and disappeared only gradually, causing Sartre much anguish.

We chose to do a presentation on Ignace Meyerson's

theories on the imagination, secretly armed with the ideas contained in the unpublished manuscript of *The Psychology of Imagination*.[12] Sartre, who always had a wonderful rapport with his former students and was very generous, gave it to us before publication. The problem is that Meyerson was one of the psychologists Sartre had shot down in his own writings. In an article on the imagination, Meyerson had written of a "new field that escapes identification." Sartre's scathing response was the following: "As if the psychologist were supposed to map uncharted lands!" As I continued with my presentation, our professor's long, pale face grew yet paler. Since I was facing the audience with my back turned to him, I did not notice. The discussion that followed showed us how broad-minded he was: it would have been easy for him to attack us, but he did not. We had shown how careless we were and how haughty; in this respect we took after our teacher, Sartre.

When I think back on that seemingly wonderful time—when we astonished people at the Sorbonne, when the four of us walked together as if we were going off to battle, when my radiance, the bold way I dressed, and my three bodyguards earned me a lot of surprised looks—when I think back on all that, I feel somewhat ashamed.

I was driven by a zeal for my work and a sort of joy that came at once from my interest in my studies and the new experience of my life as a student. My former classmates, now my friends, tell me I was voluble, flirtatious, and brilliant. At the same time, all four of us were so steeped in the "revolutionary" ideas of Sartre's phenomenology that we allowed ourselves to scorn some of our professors at the Sorbonne, to skip their classes, or to make fun of them without realizing that we were missing important experiences and knowledge.

My relationship with my "schoolmates" (as we decided to call each other) went beyond school and work. We were all good friends and really trusted one another with our ideas. Together we went to plays, art exhibits, and especially the first true film club, the Langlois at the Musée de l'Homme. This club was still learning to walk: half the time, the director would show up to tell us, stuttering, that instead of the scheduled film, we would once again see Jean Renoir's *Little Match Girl*! In that wonderful little theater on the sixth floor of the museum, we also discovered Russian cinema: Eisenstein's *Potemkin* and Pudovkin's *Storm over Asia* made a deep impression on me. We admired the great works of Griffith: *Broken Blossoms*, *The Birth of a Nation*, and *Intolerance*. We shuddered through *Nosferatu* and delighted in the spirit of Buster Keaton. These Wednesday evening outings were all my father allowed. He was always worried about my health and claimed that if you worked during the day, you had to go to bed early. Still, we would go out for coffee after the show in one of the cafés on Place du Trocadéro.

Kanapa had his eye on me and we began to flirt, but things between us didn't go any further. Raoul Lévy, on the other hand, had professed his love for me. He suffered, for even though I felt deep friendship, respect, and admiration for him, I could not imagine him ever touching me. He was very unhappy, all the more so because I often confided in him about my affair with the Beaver and later with Sartre. I was both unthinking and cruel. When I look back on it today, I feel remorseful; the only way I can now understand my attitude is to remember my extreme flirtatiousness with men and the fact that my success made my head spin. As for Bernard Lamblin, he remained silent, apparently neutral. He was friendly but made no advances and, to be honest, I did not think about him too much.

In *Letters to Sartre* the Beaver mentions getting together rather frequently with me, Raoul, Bernard, and Jean. In addition, Sartre was meeting with Jean Kanapa, who at one time had been rather seriously depressed. (We had big discussions about whether it was philosophically legitimate to force someone to see a psychiatrist!) The repercussions of the theory of freedom nearly drove our poor friend insane. Luckily, common sense won out, and Jean regained his stability. After the Occupation, he joined the Communist party and began a long and celebrated career.

The first time I saw Sartre was when, after I had asked Simone a question about the theses set forth in *The Psychology of Imagination,* she hesitated a bit and replied, "Why don't you ask Sartre yourself? He works at the Café Mousquetaires on Avenue du Maine, quite near here." Upon arriving, I scanned the nearly empty, somewhat sinister café and a saw a man sitting near the front window, writing. He greeted me very warmly. He was wearing a sort of faded blue T-shirt of questionable cleanliness. On his ill-favored face was a constellation of blackheads, but after all, I had come to ask him a question about philosophy, not to look at him. He answered me with kindness and a teacher's clear thinking; that's all that mattered. That was my first impression of the man who was so important to my friend Simone and who was to become important to me several months later.

For my Christmas vacation in 1938, I made reservations at the youth hostel halfway up Mont d'Arbois, overlooking Saint-Gervais. I had a youth hostel membership and frequently stayed at hostels for short periods of time. This time, however, I planned to stay during my school break to go skiing, my favorite sport. Simone told me the address of the little hotel in Mégève where she and Sartre would go during the winter. We agreed to meet each other there: I was simply to take the cable car to the top of Mont d'Arbois and ski down to Mégève. And that is what I did. We skied two or three times together. Neither of them had much experience; I was more used to the snow, having skied since I was a child, but my technique was still pretty rough.

I have one special memory of these athletic frolics. One afternoon, we returned to their room to dry off and warm up. We took off our thick boots and put our feet up on the radiator. I asked Sartre a question about Spinoza. His answer turned into a long discourse on Spinozistic thought, which he knew perfectly, unlike Simone. I spent New Year's Eve with them, and because I could not go up Mont d'Arbois at night and their hotel had no rooms left, they graciously offered to let me sleep in their bathtub. It was not very comfortable, but at least I had shelter. I remember that in the morning I stepped out of the bathroom and wished them a happy New Year. At first they were very surprised, but they ended up finding what I had done charming.

My relationship with Sartre dates back to this athletic and philosophical outing. From that time on, he wooed me assiduously, and we began seeing each other. I was little more than seventeen years old, and he was thirty-three. At that time I found it perfectly natural that he should pursue me and saw nothing malicious in it. Today, I can better understand the maneuver: the Beaver was highly instrumental in what happened—she was aware of her companion's need for romantic conquests. Had she not wanted me to become the object of Sartre's advances, she would not have sent me to the Café des Mousquetaires, nor would she have cooked up the encounter at Mégève. What I now think is that she not only accepted Sartre's attraction to very young women but also introduced him to some of them. I think that he was already starting to distance himself from her, at least sexually, and that she was therefore creating other, vicarious ties to him. She thought this would allow her to control her partner's new romantic relationship, thus achieving a sort of compromise between the terms of their pact—complete sexual freedom—and her own latent distress.

During the winter of 1939 and the following spring, Sartre wooed me and seemed very much in love. We met in cafés and went out together. Since it was very cold, he wore a fluffy, belted beige coat that was too tight and made him look funny: I called him "my Bear." He gave me all sorts of animal and insect names. Obviously, the name Bienenfeld immediately brings to mind "bee." So I was "my Monkey-Bee," a nickname he wrote on my copy of *The Wall*, while the previous year he had dedicated *Nausea* "To the Bee Field, respectfully." Sometimes he compared me to a shrew, which was not at all flattering. I was very attracted by his charm, spirit, kindness, and intelligence. I no longer paid attention to his ugliness; I was flattered to be pursued by a man like him. The mere fact that he was much older than

I was a point in his favor. He took great pains to seduce me, and he was successful. I think I was especially touched by his attention. No one, and certainly never a novelist, had ever told me I had beautiful eyes, nor that my slightly hunched posture (my poor father used to reprimand me constantly for not standing up straight) was touching and pleased him. To me, Sartre was a master of the language of love; he was playful, full of unexpected images. He was not satisfied just "speaking" his love; he was also a guide, a mentor. For example, when we went to an exhibit of works by Cézanne at a gallery in the Faubourg Saint-Honoré, he gave me a detailed explanation of the techniques used by the impressionist painter to give the subjects he treated weight and volume. I accepted Sartre's superiority willingly, for if he did try to train me, it was always with affection.

One day, when we were strolling through Montmartre, walking over the old, crumbling cobblestones and tasting the still present villagelike atmosphere, we stopped in what resembled a country café with a red painted façade and a large stove for heat. It became one of our special romantic places, for it was there that Sartre openly declared his love. It took fifty-one years for me to realize that that red café was one of his favorite places to bring women. That year we often heard and hummed a German song, "Bei mir bist du schön!"[13] Sartre declared it would be *our* song. In sum, just as a waiter plays the role of a waiter, Sartre played to perfection the role of a man in love. His philosophical nature and his reflections on the relationship of the Conscience and the Other in no way altered his otherwise banal behavior. What was original in this scenario was the role played by the Beaver: she conspired with him but, more importantly, her emotions were at once an incitement and a form of security. My absolute trust in her seemed to guarantee the solidity of Sartre's love.

My emotional life was therefore divided and unified at the same time: on the one hand, I was attracted to Sartre and interested in his attention and thoughtfulness; on the other hand, I still felt passion for the Beaver. We were a *threesome*. Simone de Beauvoir claims several times in her *Letters to Sartre* that I only "imagined" we were a threesome because I wanted our relationship to match the one they had had with Olga Kosakievicz and describe in their novels. By blaming me for believing we had a love triangle, she tries to minimize how much she hurt me. In fact, indirect proof of this lie can be found in Deirdre Bair's book, based on evidence given by Simone de Beauvoir:

> *Bianca quickly became entranced by Sartre, who seduced her into a brief affair during the summer of 1939 but ended it almost as soon as it began because he was frightened by her skittishness. He used Beauvoir—not for the first and certainly not for the last time—as his shield between himself and Bianca as well as his excuse for curtailing their intimacy. Nevertheless, he continued to play a game he enjoyed very much for the next several years: writing letters professing his undying love for the girl while always being careful to state that both he and Castor [i.e., the Beaver] shared the sentiment. . . . [Bianca] became, or, more accurately, wanted desperately to become, what they had desired Olga to be during their years in Rouen: the completion of their trio. But whether the couple had tired of such games or had been too badly burned by their experience with Olga*

to try to create the trio a second time, they were united in not wanting to place Bianca in such a privileged position within their lives.[14]

Yet I affirm that I never would have invented such a unique and complex arrangement myself. I was much too naïve about love then. In addition, in Sartre's letters to me (published as written to "Louise Védrine"), he states several times that there are three of us who love each other: "But there is one thing I do know well, in any case, that *our* future is *your* future; there is no difference—and that the Beaver lives in a world in which you are everywhere and always present."[15] A little later that same summer of 1939, he also wrote to me: "Do you understand, my love, even if there were a war, there would be an *afterward*, for the three of us."[16]

It is quite possible that Sartre was less serious than the Beaver, who was always more reserved in her commitments. It seems normal that he was not at all jealous of the Beaver's affection for me, while some of the Beaver's letters indicate that she was jealous of Sartre's relationship with me. That also explains why she tried to reduce to nothing our threesome when discussing these matters with Deirdre Bair. But it is undeniable that the "threesome," a complicated arrangement, was solemnly proclaimed by Sartre and Simone de Beauvoir. Thus, I believed it existed.

So deep was my belief that one day in the spring of 1939, while strolling in Paris with the Beaver through a scrap iron market near the Porte de Vanves, I was struck by a sort of vision, a blinding intuition that overcame me: I imagined that my life was written in stone, that everything had been said and nothing important would ever happen to me again. This vision seized hold of me and frightened me. Although I was only eighteen, this permanent, absolute fate was like a threat. I felt like a prisoner of the threesome. I immediately told the Beaver. This probably disturbed her deeply, for she said nothing.

After several weeks during which Sartre wooed me assiduously, it became an issue whether or not we would "consummate" our relationship; that is, Sartre made it an issue. As far as I was concerned, I had neither desire nor objection, although I did perhaps feel the thrill of a new experience. I thought it would be absurd and petty to refuse. So we chose the day, a day I will remember for the rest of my life. I already mentioned that Sartre lived in the same hotel on Rue Cels as did the Beaver. We walked up Avenue du Maine and, when we approached Rue Froidevaux, he said to me in an amused, smug manner, "The hotel chambermaid will really be surprised, because I already took a girl's virginity yesterday." I shuddered inside, but I said and did nothing. Anyone else would have turned on her heels and never come back again. I'm not shy, and I generally make a quick comeback. But I was quiet then because I was so deeply offended and because the vulgarity was so flagrant. I'll never understand why I didn't react to such boorishness, nor why Sartre saw fit to say what he did.

When we got to his room, Sartre undressed almost completely and stood by the sink to wash his feet, raising first one leg, then the other. I was intimidated. When I asked him to draw the curtains a bit to shut out some of the light, he refused flatly, saying that what we were going to do should be done in broad daylight. I hid behind the curtain of a closet to undress; I felt overwhelmed and intimidated to be naked in front of a man for the first time. I did not take off my pearl necklace, which unfortunately displeased my partner—he made fun of me because this last adornment seemed ridiculously childish to him, or maybe he was annoyed because they were natural pearls, and he was scornful of my father's business, I don't know. I was distressed and did not understand why he was not his usual, gentle self; it was as if he wanted to brutalize something in me (but also in himself) and was driven by a destructive impulse, rather than the natural desire to initiate pleasurable physical intimacy.

It was quite clear to me that he was incapable of letting himself go physically, of opening himself up to sensuality. His constantly wakeful intelligence broke all ties between his mind and his body. Anything related to the body probably seemed foreign to him. The experience I had that day reminds me of the disgust that oozes from what he wrote later, in *Paths of Freedom*: the character Mathieu, reflecting on the embryo developing inside his girlfriend's body (they have decided on an abortion), makes a bizarre comparison between a little boy who is watching him and that beginning of a life that he is casting away into the darkness: "The little creature had not long emerged from a womb, as indeed was plain: there he was, hesitant, minute, still displaying the unwholesome sheen of vomit: but behind the flickering humours that filled his eye-sockets, lurked a greedy little consciousness. . . . There was no time to lose, for the blister was expanding, at that very moment: it was making obscure efforts to emerge, to extricate itself from darkness, and growing into something like *that*, a little pallid, flabby object that clung to the world and sucked its sap."[17]

This text had not yet been published in 1939, but my contact with Sartre warned me subtly that something was wrong with the way he related to his own body and the bodies of other people. Maybe his disgust with the human body was a result of his Protestant upbringing. Or maybe this self-hatred developed the day he discovered his own ugliness. In *The Words* he explains how a few quick snips of the scissors transformed the adored blond child into a monster: "There were shrieks, but no hugging and kissing, and my mother locked herself in her room to cry. Her little girl had been exchanged for a little boy. But that wasn't the worst of it. As long as my lovely ringlets fluttered around my ears, they made it possible to deny my obvious ugliness. Yet my right eye was already entering the twilight. She had to admit the truth to herself. My grandfather himself seemed nonplussed. He had been entrusted with her little wonder and had brought back a toad."[18] Sartre's ugliness was obvious, but he always made sure people did not notice by becoming a sparkling orator and spouting off endless subtle and phenomenally intelligent ideas. Once you began listening to him, you no longer looked at him. His body was useful only insofar as it had a mouth capable of uttering truth, flattery, and lies.

I was completely on edge, terribly stiff. There was no affection to ease the situation, no truly spontaneous gesture. It seemed as if the man was following some sort of prewritten, prelearned program. It was as though he were a doctor preparing for an operation, and I had only to let myself be taken. Nothing could be accomplished that day, however: I did not let myself go, despite the painstaking efforts of my partner. Then, like a science professor, Sartre began lecturing me about the anatomy and physics of lovemaking. He was surprised that, given my contact with the Beaver, I was not better informed. In the days that followed, he achieved his goal, but I began a period of frigidity that lasted throughout our entire relationship.

This pitiful beginning makes me think of the naïve, frightened woman in Henri Michaux's marvelous poem "Bridal Night": "If, on your marriage day, returning home, you set your wife in a well to soak for the night, she will be dumbfounded. No comfort to her now that she has always had a vague uneasiness. . . . 'There now,' she will say, 'so that's what it is then, marriage. That's why they keep the manner of it so secret. I've let myself be taken in.' But being vexed, she will say nothing."[19] Because of Sartre's brutality, boorishness, coldness, and condescending pedantry, it was a long time before I could enjoy sexual relations. It took all of Bernard's love, all his warmth, and all his patience to help me overcome the shock of that disastrous first experience.

My friendship with the Beaver (as I called her from then on, since she did not like "Simone," the name her family used) continued, with its ups and downs. At the time, I had no idea that her capriciousness toward me was related to my affair with Sartre. Even though she managed to keep the threesome under control, thanks to my trustful openness with her, she had jealous moments, and the mood swings I suffered were at least partly due to the vague terror that seized hold of her whenever Sartre began a new relationship.

Not everything about our relationship was negative, however. Little by little, we renewed our physical intimacy, which I found very pleasing and captivating. Unlike Sartre, the Beaver had a comforting ability to let herself go. She seemed happy to see me and talk to me, and she was warm. Her tenderness seemed real. Of course, there was a constant attitude of domination in our relationship, on top of the disparity caused by our difference in age. She sought to mold me according to the ideas she and Sartre had adopted. But however flexible I was, it was never enough for her, and I maintained my critical nature.

For example, I accused her of not living by her own principles: since she had told me she no longer felt any friendship for Olga, I reproached her for continuing to see Olga "out of pity"—that is to say, I made her confront the contradiction between her professed moral ideas and her actions. She did not make me wait for an answer: she immediately threw it back in my face. More generally, my uneasiness stemmed from the fact that Sartre's and the Beaver's lives were too complicated, too full of various commitments. Maybe I was simply asking that they keep the promises they lavished on me, and Simone de Beauvoir must have felt slightly dizzy thinking about all the promises she had no intention of keeping. "She must be taken seriously, you know. She'll insist on every promise made to her being kept."[20]

Simone de Beauvoir was openly selfish. Where her own pleasure was at stake, nothing could deter her. To give an example, at the beginning of July 1939 I had a rather serious operation. I suffered greatly during the following days. Simone de Beauvoir came to see me at the clinic and, angry at having been "bothered" by the arrival of my parents, she wrote: "I stayed [at the clinic] for an hour and a half. Bienenfeld was well and very sweet, but her mother stuck like a burr—she did it deliberately, out of spite. When her father and sister showed up, I got the hell out—and arrived at the Flore a bit late. But I made a few jokes about Bienenfeld, which went down very well (for Olga Kosakievicz)."[21] This illustrates several of the Beaver's character traits: first, her refusal to understand that it is natural for parents to visit their daughter in the hospital—once their presence bothered her, she became resentful toward them. Second, her vulgarity and cruelty in avenging the presence of my parents by mocking me in front of Kosakievicz and Bost, telling her friends anything to make them laugh at my expense.

In order to fully appreciate what happened at the beginning of July 1939, it is important to know that, a few days after her visit to the clinic, she went to meet Bost. She and Sartre had fabricated a terrific lie to tell Olga, Wanda, and me. The Beaver was supposedly going to La Pouèze to visit "the Lady" (Madame Morel, a rich friend of hers and Sartre's). Sylvie le Bon explains this blandly in a footnote: "De Beauvoir was getting ready to visit Bost, who was doing his military service at Amiens. It was advisable for this visit to be concealed from both Olga (who was already in a relationship with Bost) and Bianca Bienenfeld. Moreover, de Beauvoir could not claim to be with Sartre at Saint-Fargeau near Saint-Saveur, since Wanda—in love with Sartre—was proving extremely jealous."[22]

To round out my recovery, my mother, sister, and I went to stay in La Clusaz, overlooking Annecy. Toward the end of July, Sartre, who had been away from Paris during my operation, wrote to try to console me after the Beaver's departure: "My love, I don't know quite what to tell you about the Beaver's departure. But there is one thing I do know, in any case, . . . that the Beaver lives in a world in which you are everywhere and always present."[23] He wanted to see me before the end of August, so he came to visit me in La Clusaz for four days. My mother was very angry when he arrived, but what could she do? Sartre stayed in another hotel, and we would hike in the mountains during the day. Mother had no way of preventing my friend from being there. Things went well, overall. But after these happy days he had to leave to meet Wanda and then the Beaver at Madame Morel's superb villa in Juan-les-Pins. I accompanied him as far as Annecy. I was sad to leave him, and before his train departed, I took two photos of him sitting on a bench near the edge of the lake.

The letters Sartre wrote me that summer and during the first few months he was a soldier were published by Simone de Beauvoir in her collections *Witness to My Life* and *Quiet Moments in a War*. These collections include tender, loving letters bursting with declarations of his affection and love for the Beaver, whose praises he was happy to sing.

In a letter from Marseille dated August 4, Sartre took it upon himself to give me an entire philosophy course, or rather he tried—as he often did—to correct some of my faults: "We then agreed that we should dissuade you from your rationalism because you have the optimistic tendency to believe that it is possible to confront irrational objects

Jean-Paul Sartre behind his automobile in July of 1939, during a visit to Annecy to see Bianca Bienenfeld.

with rational conduct."²⁴ Sartre's missives are full of detailed and often trifling descriptions of everything he does, says, and sees. Sometimes there are philosophical surprises: "After that we went to sit beneath the plane trees at Place de la Préfecture, on the terrace of a café named le Pélican. It grew dark, a mild night without streetlights, darkness falling from the trees, we could hear people going on about their lives but we couldn't see them, it was cool, it was so poetic, and we talked about philosophic reality and we became existential."[25] What does it mean to "become existential"? I still do not know. To appreciate the style of these letters and the jargon Sartre and Simone de Beauvoir used, as well as the kind of questions they discussed, it is necessary to know that their conversations were full of such expressions. For example, I was present at a discussion of their decision not to have children. How could this be justified? "And what if everyone copied us?" Indeed, Kant taught philosophers that an act was moral only if it was possible to universalize its "maxim." Thus their thought, despite its seeming immoralism, was still influenced by Kant! But the high point of their discussion occurred when, almost shocked, they concluded: "But if everyone follows our example and has no children, there won't be anyone left to read our works or anyone else's in the future." They were shattered.

Sartre loved to embellish various everyday situations. One day we were having cold drinks on the terrace of a café. He ordered a Perrier with a slice of lemon. Since I preferred another drink, he undertook to demonstrate to me that Perrier embodies a certain austerity, a bitterness, a pureness—in short, a value. Sartre was a natural at producing insipid, empty phrases. It was a sort of brilliant intellectual gymnastics in which self-satisfaction was raised to the highest degree.

He also liked to improvise. He accepted an invitation from Gabriel Marcel to give a lecture on promises. But he did not have time to reflect on the topic. In the taxi on the way to Gabriel Marcel's home on Rue Tournon, he outlined aloud the main ideas of his speech: "A free conscience cannot make promises," he explained to me, "because it cannot sign away its own future freedom; it cannot override its freedom. It follows that one can never make a promise or commit oneself." When I heard him utter these paradoxes, I thought that the conscience, according to Sartre, resembled Descartes's conception of God, whose creation is not self-sufficient: God must at every instant renew the creative act. This is the doctrine of "continuous creation," whereby time is divided into separate instants. Sartre had reduced human beings to a succession of instants in which freedom is as futile and capricious as it is fleeting. To think that several years later, after the war, he dared to develop the notion of commitment is truly a paradox. I should have paid closer attention to this refusal to make promises, a philosophical refusal that nonetheless threatened the world of emotions. I confess that, at the time, this thought did not cross my mind.

TWO

The War

The three of us were apart when the war broke out. The emotional drama that was to involve us thus took place against the backdrop of war. Toward the end of August, my father, who was with us in Annecy, was called up to join a medical corps unit in Melun. That was the first time an administrative authority recognized my father's medical degrees (although he was only a medical auxiliary). He left us, advising Mother to go to Quimper, to our friends the Perraults. My mother bravely took the wheel and drove us across France from east to west. Sometimes she became so tired that she told me not to fall asleep, so I could stay alert by her side. The second morning, as we were going through a village in the Auvergne, we saw a crowd gathered near the city hall. Having guessed what was happening, we stopped and read the notice of general mobilization. It was September 2; the mobilization decree had been signed September 1. Although the newspapers had bombarded us with clichés such as "mobilization is not war," people knew better. There were mostly women standing near the notice, crying. Many men had already left. Heavyhearted, we got back on the road. We settled in Quimper to watch and wait for war, a war we could scarcely imagine and which scared us to death. My mother took a nursing exam so she could help out at the hospital. I took typing courses so I could work, if necessary, for no one knew how long the army would keep Father, who was forty-six years old.

Sartre and the Beaver returned to Paris, they too finally worried about the turn of events. At the end of August, Sartre wrote me again, to "calm my nerves": "And yet I would have liked to reassure you. I can scarcely endure the idea of leaving without seeing you again. . . . But listen, perhaps I never thought to tell you: I am *not in any danger*. . . . Almost a shirker, if you get my drift. Just remember, I'm a meteorologist. . . . For that matter, I don't really believe in the war. Obviously this letter runs the risk of arriving at the same moment as the announcement of general mobilization."[1] In another letter he dared to write, "It is impossible that Hitler is thinking of starting a war, given the mental state of the German population. . . . To be an altogether, altogether perfect little Louise [Védrine, pseudonym used for my name], you must resist the tendency toward jeremiads and be totally calm."[2]

It wasn't just another war—everyone but the pacifists understood that. It was a war driven by Hitler. Nazism pervaded all aspects of our lives during those prewar years and, of course, during the war and the Occupation. It is shocking that Sartre was apparently never fully aware of how severe the threat of Nazism was for Europe. After all, he had spent a year in Berlin beginning in autumn 1933, the same year that Hitler was officially named chancellor of the Reich.

Perhaps I'm being too harsh. He probably had his worries, and, in any case, he was certainly very hostile toward such a regime. I think he was simply so absorbed in philosophy, so smitten by Husserl, that the significance of historical events could not penetrate his intellectual world.

The difficulties in my relationship with Sartre were caused primarily by his general prewar attitude concerning political reality and history. It is now well known that he and the Beaver were rather unaware of the social and political world around them. They later confessed this simply and honestly. Their stance was vaguely anarchist, more by instinct than by doctrine. The first reason for their lack of awareness was their all-consuming, selfish intellectual ambition, their drive to succeed as writers, which absorbed them completely. The second was that, like many French writers, they lived in a vacuum: surrounded by Parisian friends, they had no contact with the rest of the world and led a sort of "cliquish" existence. The third is perhaps that philosophy is not history: philosophy doesn't prepare people to plunge into the world of current events but rather to glide above it, to observe it with an eagle's eye. Sartre's big breakthrough occurred while he was in prison—at least that is how he describes his own development.

Even before the war the gap between him and me, or between them and me, was already very wide. Not because I joined a political party—I have never had the desire to do so—but because I was Jewish, and that obviously made me very sensitive to what was happening in the world, ever since I was a child. My father was already "on the left"; he must have influenced me unconsciously. I was fifteen when the Spanish Civil War broke out, and I followed each stage of that war with fascination. I was dismayed at how little support the republicans received from France and Britain; I resented the bitter antagonism between the Spanish communists and anarchists. And the two-faced politics of the USSR, which claimed to support the republican government but did not send the aid it needed, deeply disgusted me and caused my stubborn mistrust of communism. We were visited by a distant Polish cousin who fought in the International Brigade and returned from the front injured both physically and emotionally. It was therefore natural that I should take an interest in that civil war, the prelude to the Second World War. I tried to help the victims as much as I could, for example, by becoming involved with the Quakers, who had a radio station in the Sixteenth Arrondissement.

But de Beauvoir was not completely unaware; she just worked hard at repressing her knowledge. In *The Prime of Life* she relates the story I told her of one of my German Jewish cousins who had been tortured, burned with cigarettes. She writes: "Bianca Bienenfeld was visited by one of her cousins. . . . He had been beaten up for hours on end. . . . 'How can anyone still work and play and carry on his life as usual when things like *that* are being done?' Bianca asked me, weeping. And I, who was so obstinately determined to stake everything on happiness, felt ashamed of my egocentricity. Yet despite my shame I still did not abandon my position, still tried hard to believe that there would be no war."[3]

The protective tone of the letters Sartre wrote me that summer of 1939 was hard to bear. These letters show just how caught up he was in his lies and illusions regarding the conflict that was about to occur. He pretends to believe that I was worried only about what harm might befall him. But I had bigger things to worry about.

This led to a serious misunderstanding between us: he knew I was very frightened of what was to come and what might happen to me and all the Jews. He saw my extreme anguish and assumed the role of an older brother who must, at all costs, talk sense into his little sister and calm her down. In several of his letters he tried to appease me with vain, empty words. I was much more aware than he of what was occurring, and with good reason. Because of this, his efforts to console me seemed pathetic and only irritated me, despite his good intentions.

Sartre wrote things that now seem (and seemed at the time) utterly ridiculous: "For that matter, I don't really believe in the war. . . . The German people seem anything but enthusiastic. If you ask me, the big blow was to have been struck on Friday or Saturday at the latest: as he announced the German-Soviet pact, Hitler was counting on disarray among the democracies and internal troubles in France. . . . Bear in mind that the point of view I have just put forth is the one shared by everyone here. . . . Obviously, there is still the possibility of 'bullshit.'. . . My love, I swear to you that what torments us the most these days is the concern you are feeling."[4] But on September 2 he had no choice but to recognize that "the bullshit triumphed. I'm leaving tonight at five o'clock."[5]

Sartre was not the only one who was blind to how serious things were for France, Europe, and the Jews; indeed, such an attitude was very common at the time. After all, the French were raised to believe that their country was strong (hadn't France won the Great War?) and had a powerful army. No one could imagine the possibility of victory for the troops of the Third Reich. Strangely, this confidence was mixed with traditional French pacifism, a stance reinforced by the horrors of the First World War. Some libertarian circles expressed this rejection of war with characteristic slogans: "Servitude rather than war." "The traditional pacifists found altogether unexpected allies in the wholehearted nationalists," writes the contemporary historian Jean-Pierre Azéma.[6] Some were inspired by fear that a new war would cause ideological upheaval similar to that which had occurred in the Soviet Union. Others, however, were motivated by socialist or anarchist leanings. Therefore, Sartre and Simone de Beauvoir's lack of awareness was not due simply to their own idiosyncracies but reflected the widespread faintheartedness of French people from all walks of life.

In fact, I did not worry too much about Sartre's safety, despite the unforeseeable circumstances that, during a war, could endanger people at the front as well as behind the lines, both fighting troops and civilians. What was painful was being far away from him. In any case, one thing was certain: a Nazi victory would spell grave danger for the Jews. Neither Sartre nor de Beauvoir ever said a word about that. It is as if they had never known, or wanted to forget, that this put me directly in the line of fire, so to speak. But the most shocking evidence of their indifference is the simple fact that first one, then the other, broke up with me, stopped "loving" me, in 1940, the year of all those disasters. They left me. France had been defeated, and the repercussions were frightening. The combination of these events brought on the severe trauma I suffered. Their decision and their persistent refusal to accept any responsibility toward me is quite revealing, both with regard to their selfishness and their lack of awareness. From the end of 1940 until the Liberation I remained completely cut off from them. They never worried about my fate or tried to get news of me.

I shall now return to the story of the first months of that "phony war." Once settled into our meager surroundings in Quimper, we waited to see what would happen. Since there were no significant attacks, we began to wonder what we were doing there. Around September 20 the Beaver came to see me, as she explains in *Letters to Sartre* and *The Prime of Life*.[7] That was a deeply moving moment for me, spoiled by my mother's rather violent scenes; she was furious that Simone de Beauvoir had come to see me even in our Breton refuge. Mother was very worried that my attachment to my former teacher was still alive and becoming deeper. Her hot temper also made her jealous, as she had been of all my female friends. My father was angry, of course, but he could tell when action would be useless and even counterproductive. He had understood that my determination was irrepressible and thus spared me useless reproaches. Actually, both my parents realized how deeply enmeshed I was, but I refused to see it, refused to hear anything of it. In any case, I could not have cared less what they thought and was prepared to do anything, even leave them, if they tried to stop me. They were therefore absolutely powerless.

It was time for me to think about going back to school. In October I took a small room in the university residence hall in Rennes. That was my first room all to myself away from home. I was thrilled with my new independence. I had escaped the criticism of my overprotective mother and was able to devote myself fully to my studies. In class and at the library I saw one of my classmates, Pierre Guastalla—we called him Pierrot—whom I had barely seen at the Sorbonne. His father was a talented painter and engraver, and his mother, a physicist, was intelligent and kindhearted. A bit younger than I, he was highly ambitious and had many talents. He wrote philosophical studies but also wanted to write plays, essays, and novels. His mind was full of projects and ideas. He was an enthusiastic, open, very charming person. During the two months I stayed in Rennes, we built a solid friendship. We would work together, go to concerts and cafés, and spend a lot of time discussing philosophy. Pierrot had a passion for phenomenology, and my ties to Sartre made a big impression on him.

During the All Saints' Day vacation I made a quick jaunt to Paris to see the Beaver. My visit with her was tense and unhappy; we fought often. She seemed to spend time with me grudgingly and couldn't conceal her uneasiness. Something had come between us, without my suspecting it. "If she comes back to Paris, it will be a real little cataclysm—a disaster for me," wrote the Beaver in a letter to Sartre.[8] In my blindness, I was unaware of what was happening and couldn't wait to be with her again. The Beaver's life and the life she made me lead were very complicated, because she divided her time among Olga Kosakievicz, Nathalie Sorokine—also a student from Lycée Molière, in the class after mine—and me. Her everyday world revolved exclusively around women, as was the case for many women during the war. Her men—Sartre, whom she placed above all the rest, and Bost, with whom she was madly in love—were far away: she could maintain ties with them only through letters or by taking advantage of their periods of leave, which were hard to predict. I had no idea she loved Little Bost, since she deliberately lied to me about him. It was only when we broke up, nearly a year later, that she confessed her growing attachment to him.

Sartre wrote a great deal: to the Beaver every day, to me two or three times a week, to his mother once a week, surely also to Wanda and who knows how many others. It was understood that the Beaver and I would exchange our letters to spare Sartre the chore of having to repeat himself. This was a way for him to save a little time, given his remarkable desire to write to all "his" women: he related *everything* in minute detail—his day-to-day life, his sometimes comical relations with his meteorology chums at work, his thoughts and desires. He described his progress in writing *The Age of Reason* and the evolution of his philosophical thought, for he was already developing the main ideas of *Being and Nothingness*. I therefore naïvely showed the Beaver the letters Sartre sent me, never wondering how the declarations of love that filled them made her feel. She showed me the equally loving letters he sent her. At the time I had no doubt she showed me everything. Now I am sure she did not.[9]

I was also unaware that her struggle against me began at that time. I did have a vague inkling of her big change of heart, however: she was strangely capricious, one minute friendly and loving, the next irritated and critical of my behavior or my thoughts. I suffered through her moods, having no idea that they might have stemmed from her jealousy toward me. I attributed them to her painful separation from Sartre and to the worries the war caused us. In her daily letters to Sartre, she would of course describe every event of her life in Paris, big or small, in rich detail. It is therefore possible to trace both the complexities of her feelings and her worries (about money, for instance) in those difficult times. The only thing to remember—and this is very important—is that her stories about what she does and the thoughts she describes concerning her friendships and hesitations are most certainly fabricated, exaggerated. I realized this only gradually, shocked by salacious statements and fanciful details. It was then that I understood that the reality she wished to present to Sartre at the time was supposed to entertain him, amuse him, or excite him sexually. It was all part of the "big voyeuristic game," and it would be a big mistake to trust blindly what Simone de Beauvoir writes simply because she wrote it.

The biggest shock for me in reading *Letters to Sartre* was discovering how she became annoyed with me and later secretly decided to push me away, insidiously leading Sartre to break with me first to achieve her goal. I have no choice but to recognize that she was the one behind it all: she created a more and more displeasing image of me. She explained which arguments to use, which strategy to adopt in order to justify breaking up with me. I thought then and for all the years that followed that Sartre alone was responsible for the brutal letter I received at the end of February 1940. At the time, I turned to the Beaver for sympathy and consolation. Only fifty years later did I realize that she was the one who had pulled the strings in that pathetic affair. It is

Simone de Beauvoir on the terrace of Saint-Germaine-en-Laye in the spring of 1938.

quite obvious that I turned to her at the beginning of 1945, hoping to rebuild our friendship, because I was completely convinced she had had nothing to do with Sartre's behavior toward me. More than forty years of what I believed to be sincere friendship were thus destroyed, reduced to nothing in one blow.

"Sartre would like to break with Védrine gently. I don't think he can, but I'm done worrying and feeling bitter for nothing. I'm not afraid of anything. I'm tangled up with Sartre once again, alone with him as in the days of Le Havre or Rouen before Kos. . . . So I'm happy."[10] In so many words in her *Journal de guerre*, Simone de Beauvoir exposes the jealousy she had carefully concealed until then and her desire to have the man of her life all to herself, rather than share him with others against her will, as she had before. My presence must have worried her to the point of exposing her "joy at being alone with him" in this manner. Having Sartre all to herself was probably her main motive, the concern beneath the growing disgust she claims to have felt toward me.

But there was another motive, linked to my own strong feelings. The core of this increasingly bitter conflict lay in our obviously different interpretations of the threesome. According to Simone de Beauvoir's letters, it was apparently *my* idea to divide our relationship into three equal parts. This perspective irritated her, and she immediately perceived it as a serious threat. In her letter dated November 12, she relates a long dispute on this sticky subject. If indeed I did, as she writes, claim to share Sartre equally with her, I clearly—at the very least—had no sense of psychology, especially since the Beaver suffered from Sartre's distance and infrequent periods of leave. She describes this lively discussion to him at length: "She began to reproach me for not wanting to leave you to her for 6 days during your leave. Flushing with anger, I told her I couldn't understand how she envisaged our relations; that she seemed to see the threesome as an exact tripartite division, which astonished me. . . . I said she was mistaken—that things wouldn't be like that—and for a moment there was a real, sharp quarrel. . . . She sobbed, but then calmed down. . . . She also remembered that until August she'd seen the threesome as a base made up of you and me, with a projecting point that was her, rather than as something perfectly symmetrical."[11] Personally, I have no clear memory of the content of these rows, but it seems likely to me that my demands had increased and I had lost sight of what was real or possible—love had simply made me lose my head. The combination of the alarm caused by the war, the separation from Sartre, and the Beaver's own ambiguous attitude had probably exacerbated my interpretation of the "threesome." I had forgotten to factor in how violent she became when threatened; I had forgotten her ferocious will to keep Sartre's "necessary" love for herself, and I was unaware of her absolute power over him. As early as December 17 she discussed with him the possibility of breaking with me: "With respect to your hopes regarding Bienenfeld, I think they're fruitless. Unconsummated craving is as fearsome as the other kind, and it binds her tight. So when she sees you again, she'll be utterly smitten. Especially with sexuality involved, that won't take long. If you want to stop the affair, that may be possible without a *disaster*—but not without a fuss. It would take a lot of toughness, moreover: diminish the passion in your letters, say a cool farewell, etc."[12]

Her undermining efforts continued: "I don't know if I should tell you the whole story of my evening yesterday, since—out of solidarity—it'll finish off Bienenfeld in your eyes. I've never felt so chilled by her. . . . I hate her little jokes and her sprightliness and her gentle authority. . . . She'll never ask a question about, for example, my real feelings for Kos., or my relations with Sorokine."[13] Simone de Beauvoir's insincerity here is clear: each time I asked her about her friends she dodged the question. And I had no reason to ask her about Kosakievicz or Sorokine, my direct rivals, only to hear her lies. At the end of December she interceded again: "The extract from Bienenfeld's letter [Sartre had sent her a copy of one of my letters] doesn't strike me as all that lukewarm, or all that empty. She certainly loves you with all her heart—at least intermittently. . . . I'm sorry to have put you off her so much, but that's pretty well how I feel myself."[14]

In February 1940 the Beaver, who seems to have changed her tone, related a long conversation we had at the Hoggar café: "It must be said she was moving: all restrained, serious, attentive and silent, smiling at me every so often—and every so often restraining her tears. What's more, she was beautiful yesterday. It struck me as rotten, thinking of the blow that was about to fall on her head."[15] Indeed, at the end of the month, without notice, I suddenly received Sartre's letter declaring that everything was over between us. No valid reason was given. The only argument he mentioned was that the distance had "dried up" his feelings for me (but his feelings for the Beaver and Wanda had, of course, not suffered the same sad fate). The shock was even worse because it was totally unexpected; all the preceding letters had been warm, loving, romantic. Nothing that had occurred between us could have allowed me to predict such a sudden rupture. I was deeply bewildered, unable to understand. But soon after, my distress was augmented by a blow to my self-esteem. It felt like a slap in the face, not only painful but also humiliating. I wondered what to make of all the love letters I had received week after week, one of them just three days earlier, if love could dissolve in an instant like a bad dream. I understood that the feelings Sartre claimed to have had for me were nothing but empty words, a pathetic act. But why did he see fit to put on such an act? My dignity was shattered as though he had taken me for a slut, for whom a semblance of love is enough.

In Simone de Beauvoir's correspondence dated February 27, 1940, there is a long narrative of my reactions and her own. I cannot quote everything, but here are some excerpts: "She read your letters, she restrained herself with astounding guts—but she was transfigured by anger. And honestly, I don't know what got into your head. That letter, with its moral exhortations and protestations of esteem, was quite unacceptable. . . . Bienenfeld felt it that way, and tore every sentence apart with gusto. And she was humiliated that you didn't even take the trouble to explain things to her properly. Humiliated and disgusted by the passionate letters you were writing her only a fortnight earlier. I found it desperately unpleasant."[16]

Thus, despite her regrets as to the circumstances, the Beaver had achieved her goal—detaching Sartre from me—and she could feel both relieved at having eliminated the "danger" I represented and free to get rid of me herself, when the time came. From that time on, she could easily play the kind soul who for a moment sides with the victim, forgetting that she was the one who had stirred everything up. Her vulgarity was such that she later wrote, "The only thing I still reproach you with is having dispatched Bienenfeld a bit summarily—but that's unimportant."[17] Two weeks later, she concludes, "She's prophesying doom like a Cassandra (what's new?) and hesitating between the concentration camp and suicide, with a preference for suicide: she calls this sensing her destiny. I've been delighted about your rupture, since on my own I find I've incredibly much more freedom where she's concerned."[18]

Sartre came home on leave in mid-April. This time I got word of it beforehand and was allowed to receive my dismissal face to face, as I had asked. We were to meet in a café on Place du Trocadéro. I tried hard not to cry but wasn't entirely successful. I demanded to know what he had been thinking that made him change so suddenly from loving to feeling nothing. That painful conversation was as empty as his letters. The only unexpected thing was another incidence of his boorish behavior. Probably wanting to say something nice, Sartre mumbled just before leaving, "What consoles me is that I'm sure you'll get over it." Those were the exact words Simone de Beauvoir had used. This "certainty" of theirs worked to their advantage and spared them from having to face the seriousness of their actions. The fact that Sartre consoled himself by imagining I was strong enough to withstand the pain he caused me was like a second slap in the face I could well have done without. Sartre's selfishness was probably less apparent than the Beaver's, but his feelings were more superficial, allowing his selfishness to show through his awkward comments. Most of all, his extreme boorishness, lack of sensitivity, flippancy, and irresponsibility hurt me more than a slow and natural change in his feelings would have.

During the three years of our first friendship I never perceived in the Beaver the least bit of disgust at my being Jewish. Besides, I myself was in no way obsessed with the widespread anti-Semitism of other people, as were many Jews who believed all "goys" were anti-Semitic. Even though I had now and again suffered various insults, especially at the lycée, I would never have imagined that someone who claimed to be my friend could succumb to racism. Maybe I am the one who was deaf and blind. Moreover, I never had any doubts: after the war, de Beauvoir and Sartre openly and permanently took the side of the Jews and Israel.

That is what made it so painful to discover entire passages in the *Letters* in which the Beaver elaborates on my Jewishness, painting my portrait using muddled psychology with references drawn from the most hackneyed clichés peddled by the European anti-Semitic tradition. "We had another long conversation about authenticity. I was suddenly struck by Védrine's 'devout Jewishness' and the way she had never been a child but always a little grown-up, caught up in the social whirlwind since childhood, living *with* it and not against it as children usually do—partly because of her upbringing, but mostly because of her rather monstrous intelligence."[19] What did she know of my childhood? Me, a devout Jew? I was not devout in the least; I had not the slightest inclination to worship any God whatsoever. She was more likely to be devout, given her childhood. In what way is my intelligence monstrous? What about theirs? The philosophy of Heidegger, more or less well accepted during that probationary time, had gone to her head. She attacked me constantly for my "inauthenticity," a term borrowed from Heidegger's vocabulary. The Beaver believed it was an existential crime to live equally in social and historic reality. She also scolded me quite often for being "rational," because being authentic probably meant being irrational, like a character out of Wagner. In Germany, Nazism had spawned a cult of instinct, of deep, unexplained urges. Jews were constantly accused of being too rational. The philosophy of Heidegger is partially responsible for the peddling of these twisted ideas. The discussions we had about these subjects left a bad taste in my mouth, but I wasn't really sure why and couldn't defend myself very well.

The most "telling" passage, the one that sheds the most light on the sources of her psychological imagination, is dated December 10, 1939, in *Journal de guerre*: "I explained to her that for her it's always a matter of 'making a profit,' of 'making a good investment'; but in the end life is only for living. Védrine is interested in personal gain but without knowing exactly what it means to be a person. To explain personal gain from the bottom up, social success is on the horizon, but in a way social standing is for her a guarantee of the metaphysical objectivity of reality and values. That is undoubtedly the kind of compassion she has, and the mishmash of excessive desperation and solidity: she weeps before a wailing wall that she diligently builds with her own hands, that she builds often to protect the positive wealth she bitterly seeks to defend. Something like the old Jewish usurer who weeps with pity for the client he has driven to suicide."[20]

Here is the age-old Jewish miser stereotype, and I'm mixed up with it! Soon all of Europe would be covered by an enormous "wailing wall" that the Jews most certainly did not build! The war was in full swing, and all Simone de Beauvoir could find to say about me is that I like money, as do all Jews. The truth is that such ideas and images resurfaced from her upbringing. She had reputedly condemned her family's ideas, especially the obsessions of her father, who had always been a notorious anti-Semite and was even more so during the war, something the Beaver never told me: "The only topic that animated [Simone de Beauvoir's father] was the establishment of several agencies which he hoped would finally rid France of the Jews, whom he held responsible for the ills that had befallen the country."[21] This reveals the contradiction between her conscious ideas, which were probably not anti-Semitic, and the moldy tradition of a family of petty, proper French nobles who blamed their decay on the Jews. These thoughts made her attitude toward me increasingly critical.

What is most incredible is that in 1990, when I reread *The Age of Reason*, the novel Sartre wrote during the "funny little war," I found disturbing similarities to expressions used by Simone de Beauvoir in her *Letters to Sartre*. The first Jewish character we encounter in this novel is an abortionist:

> *"Yes, I do: [I know] just the person—why didn't I think of it before? Waldmann. You haven't met him here? A Jew, a gynecologist. He's a sort of specialist in abortion."*

> ... "I'm terribly sorry," said Sarah's voice: "but he wants four thousand francs, cash down. I did tell him that you were rather hard up at the moment, but he wouldn't budge. He's a dirty Jew," she added with a laugh.²²

That despicable abortionist is, of course, portrayed as grasping for money.

And so begins the transfer of vocabulary and images from the Beaver's letters to the novel Sartre was then writing [*The Reprieve*]. "The Babylonian exile, the curse on Israel, and the wailing wall, the destinies of the Jewish nation had not altered."²³ Then we meet Monsieur Birnenschatz, the diamond merchant, and his daughter, Ella, as well as several other characters, although it is rather unclear why they are introduced. The scene is set as follows:

> *Ella Birnenschatz clasped her thin brown arms round her father's neck.* "Papa, you are a darling," *said Ella Birnenschatz.* . . . "You're making me all wet," *said M. Birnenschatz.* . . . *The mother was fat and flaccid, with a timid and appealing look in her wide eyes, which got on his nerves, but Ella took after him.* . . . *She [Ella] had made herself what she was by her life in Paris. I always say: Race?—what do you mean by race? Would you take Ella for a Jewess if you met her in the street?*
>
> ". . . *He released her, took a jewel-case off the desk, and gave it to her.* "Here you are," *he said. And he added, while she was looking at the pearls:* "Next year they'll be twice as large." . . . *Schalom* . . . *thought:* "She looks too intelligent; that's how our people are made." . . . *M. Birnenschatz thought of the pearls and said to himself:* "Not a bad investment."²⁴

The theme of money-loving Jews continues, but another—that of the desire for assimilation—is added. There are Jews such as Birnenschatz who don't want to recognize they are Jews, while Weiss, called to serve his country as a captain, sees things much differently. He tries to be honest:

> *"For us [the war] is not such damned foolishness." "For us?" asked M. Birnenschatz in astonishment. "For us? Whom are you talking about?" Weiss lowered his eyes. "For us Jews," he said. "After what they did to the Jews in Germany, we have a reason for fighting." M. Birnenschatz took a few steps; he was annoyed. "What's all this—us Jews?" he asked. "Don't know 'em. I'm French myself. Do you feel like a Jew? . . . But what is a Jew? It's a man whom other men take for a Jew."*[25]

This is the central theme of Sartre's short work *Anti-Semite and Jew*,[26] surprising though it may seem as early as 1939, in the middle of the war and in the midst of Nazism. He kept these ideas carefully hidden until later, only to pull them out of his hat like a magician, with the best intentions in the world. Strange though it may seem, the Jew who claims he is not Jewish but French like everyone else, and who declares a Jew is someone other people call a Jew, is described in *The Reprieve* in such a disagreeable, insulting manner as to confuse the reader. Does Sartre portray Birnenschatz as disagreeable in order to say that Jews must not only recognize themselves as Jews but also accept being part of the "Jewish people"? I confess that the logic of his thought completely escapes me. Either the Jews truly exist, or they are nothing but a reflection of anti-Semitic hatred: you have to choose.[27]

I would also like to point out that Sartre allows himself to use my family—clearly recognizable—in the novel he is writing, even though he hasn't yet broken with me: the name Birnenschatz is strangely similar to Bienenfeld; my sister's name is Ela; Ella's father is a diamond merchant, while my father sold natural pearls. But the Beaver's letters are the main source of some passages, including the reference to the "wailing wall" and the Beaver's statement regarding my "rather monstrous intelligence." Truly, I would call *their* intelligence monstrous and at the same time downright feeble. Sartre doesn't have much imagination or inspiration—he builds his novel from odds and ends. Already, several years before I asked them to eliminate any reference to what happened among us from their work, the evil had been done in cold, perfect literary style. My obsessive fear of being used as fodder for their writing was therefore well founded. After our breakup, I dreaded the idea that after abandoning me they could still squeeze juicy details out of what had happened among us and use them in their novels.

I worked a lot that spring. As a matter of fact, the more unhappy I feel, the more I work. And my history of philosophy course was very interesting. Jean Kanapa, Raoul Lévy, Bernard, and I faithfully attended classes given by Emile Bréhier and especially by Jean Wahl, who taught us new ways of looking at things. Even though Wahl was a very poor teacher—burying his nearsighted nose into the muddled pages he riffled through, making his voice almost inaudible—even though he always wore old castoffs too big for his small body, we found his lessons fascinating. His extensive knowledge of Greek culture and above all his familiarity with contemporary German philosophy were a welcome change from the usual Sorbonne material. He spoke to us of Kierkegaard, Jaspers, Heidegger, and Hegel. Like an echo, his lessons brought us back to phenomenology, our starting point.

We worked hard, both on our own and as a group at the Café Petit Biard at the end of Boulevard Saint-Michel. We met students from the year ahead of us: Claude Simonnet, Roland Caillois, and Yvonne Picard. We also met several École Normale students who deigned to go to the Sorbonne, including Desanti and Cuzin.

On May 10 I had to give a presentation in Bréhier's class on *dianoia* (thinking) and *noesis* (intelligence) in Plato's *Republic*. I stayed up late the night before. At nine o'clock the class began. In perfect military style as usual, Bréhier said a few words, then yielded the floor. I dove into my presentation and was soon completely absorbed in my difficult topic. But I had a vague inkling that my audience wasn't as calm as it should have been. Even my friends were moving around and chatting. When I had finished, I went down from the podium and joined them. "You must not know the news," they said. "German troops invaded Holland last night, and now they're spreading into Belgium." Then I understood why the abstract notions of Platonistic philosophy had failed to grab my audience's attention.

The month that followed left us stunned and overwhelmed. Like most French people, accustomed to the patriotic lies trumpeted by the press and by our leaders, we believed the French army to be the strongest in the world, at least strong enough to contain the troops of the Third Reich. We had no idea of the strength of the enemy's armies and especially of their tanks, and we were unaware how completely disorganized our own army was. Little by little, we discovered to our dismay that defeat was possible, maybe inevitable. I still remember how shocked I was when, upon exiting the Metro at the Duroc station about three weeks later, I heard the newspaper vendors yell, "Arras and Amiens have fallen!" The German armies had thus arrived at the gates of Paris before we could catch our breath.

My mother and sister returned to Quimper. My father wanted to stay in Paris as long as possible, in order to organize his things and prepare his departure. As for me, my friends, most of the other students, and the Beaver, we were there because we were still caught up in our studies, getting ready for exams. Simone de Beauvoir writes about the atmosphere of this period in *The Prime of Life*. In writing this book she drew from the journal she kept daily and which was recently published. I see no need to repeat what she has written. The strongest feeling I had—what gripped me constantly—was fear that the world would end. During the short time between my feeling the desire to leave, my urge to flee the invasion, and my actual departure—during that calm before the storm—I looked at the Paris I so love with the sadness of someone about to be separated from her loved one forever. I was sure Paris would be bombed, destroyed, that nothing of its beauty would remain. "Look, take it all in, look," said the executioner to Michel Strogoff.

The Beaver was very upset about being apart from Sartre,

regardless of whether she stayed or left. I obviously did not share her worry: I was upset to be going far away from her and my friends for an indefinite period. Everything seemed so uncertain, so confused. We were crushed by the reality of defeat. Finally, my father and I decided to leave Paris by car. I asked Father if we could take the Beaver with us, since she had no one to leave with. He hesitated a long time because of his well-founded animosity and mistrust toward my friend, but whether he felt sorry for her or was incapable of resisting my request, he accepted. We sat and waited for her on the terrace of the Café Mahieu, that superb café at the end of Rue Soufflot, by Place Médicis. We were stunned to see huge wagons—each carrying an entire rural family, their animals, grandmothers, and infants—slowly traveling up Boulevard Saint-Michel. They were coming from the Porte de la Chapelle to the north and heading toward the Porte d'Orléans, hoping to escape the enemy armies. That sad procession across Paris of rural people who had probably never before been to the city seemed to symbolize the end of all our hopes, all the illusions with which we had been raised. But at the same time it signified the historic revival of people's ancestral instinct to flee military invasion. At that point, when I saw that obvious sign of disaster, I cried bitterly.

In *The Prime of Life* Simone de Beauvoir writes:

> *I felt the German advance as a personal threat. There was only one idea in my head: not to be cut off from Sartre, not to be caught like a rat in occupied Paris. . . . [Bianca] told me her father had heard from some friend of his at GHQ that a big withdrawal would almost certainly take*

place the following day: all examinations were canceled and teachers released from duty. My heart froze. This was the end, and no mistake: the Germans would enter Paris within the next two days, and there was nothing for me to do but leave with her for Angers. In addition Bianca told me that the Maginot Line was obviously going to be bypassed. I realized that Sartre would be a prisoner indefinitely; that he would suffer the most appalling sort of existence, and that I would have no real news of him. For the first time in my life I had a kind of hysterical fit; this, as far as I was concerned, was the most awful moment in the whole course of the war.[28]

In *Journal de guerre* I discovered a passage describing our common exodus in an unpleasant tone, very different from that of *The Prime of Life*. Describing an alert that forced us to get out of the car on the outskirts of Chartres, she writes with scorn, "We went downstairs, too. Mr. Védrine [Bienenfeld] was holding a fancy handkerchief containing all his pearls from his business."[29]

The Beaver was so distressed at the idea that she was going to be separated from Sartre and that his life was perhaps in danger that she repeated several times in the car, "Why don't they stop all of this? Why don't they call an armistice? What good is all this slaughter?" These questions infuriated me, and we started to quarrel. I could not tolerate her feeble pacifism, inspired only by personal considerations, when the entire country was in danger. There was an essential difference between us: I was in tune with the historic significance of events; I had a clear understanding of the choice that had to be made at the time and that General de Gaulle made several days later. The Beaver was childishly selfish and totally blind to the future, believing in a sort of individualistic anarchy that was the most fertile ground for confusion and panic. Our vehement dispute symbolized perfectly the conflict that cut France in two at the crucial moment.

The trip continued without incident. After Chartres there were few people on the road. We left the Beaver at Laval, from which point she was to travel to La Pouèze and the house of her friend Madame Morel, an opulent, comfortable home where she and Sartre were always received magnificently. She was welcomed cordially; they tried to comfort her, to help her restore her shattered nerves. And, as she relates in *The Prime of Life*, it was there that she heard Pétain's speech of June 17, which made her sick because of his "paternal and militaristic" voice. But, she added, "I was relieved to learn that the shedding of French blood would cease at last: how absurd and ghastly these so-called rearguard actions were, in which men died to maintain a mere pale shadow of resistance!"[30] Then, concerned about being back in Paris in the hope of receiving news of Sartre, she went back toward the end of June.

When we arrived in Quimper, we found my mother in an extremely nervous state. There was a strained atmosphere between Mother and our friends, the Perraults. The Perraults' two sons had been captured, and there was no news of them. It was only normal that their parents be very worried. My mother was herself worried, and this resulted in a sort of animosity between the old friends. Later, the Perraults learned that Jean, their older son, had been captured in the Dunkirk pocket and taken to an officers' camp in Germany. They knew nothing about Robert, their other son. At the end of July, after we had returned to Paris, Robert came back one morning. He and some other captured officers had escaped from a holding camp in France right before they were to be transferred to Germany. We housed and clothed him and acted as a steppingstone for him and his friends into the free zone.

In Quimper we followed the news with concern. We knew that the German troops were continuing the Occupation full force. My father realized he had made a mistake in seeking refuge in the "Breton hideout," which could be surrounded. He tried to take us further south by crossing the Loire at Nantes, but while en route we learned that the Germans had beat us there and all the Loire bridges were mined. Gloomily, we turned back. Rommel's Panzers reached Cherbourg, then Brest and Lorient. The Germans had to take these essential arsenals as quickly as possible in order to prevent any contact between France and England. On June 20 vanguards of the German troops entered Quimper. It was a dramatic entry, a well-ordered parade with the blond, close-shaven scouts in the front, sitting up straight on their motorcycles, proud to represent the new Nationalist-Socialist Germany.

For the Bretons and for me, that was our first contact with the army of occupation, something new and threatening. I was extremely nervous and furious to see the people of Quimper on the sidewalks or on their balconies, watching curiously—perhaps admiringly—those superb young men on their steeds. I would have preferred the city to act as if it were dead, all the shutters closed and the shops locked up. Just watching the military parade seemed revolting to me. My parents, worried that I was overreacting, decided to send me away. They asked Monsieur Perrault, who said he knew a family in Elliant, a village twenty kilometers outside of Quimper. They could take me in. He drove me there. That was the first time I had actual contact with Breton farmers and with any sort of peasant lifestyle.

Monsieur and Madame Lennon were poor peasants who did not have full ownership of their land. During the summer they worked about fifteen hours a day. They had nine children and were expecting the tenth. They lived in the most rudimentary sort of farmhouse: dirt floor, no running water (there was a well), no electricity (carbide lamps were used for light), not even a stove (the lard and potatoes we had at each meal were boiled in a cauldron hung above the hearth). I had never lived in such conditions, but the family's simple, warm welcome helped me to adapt quickly. They called me Blanche, which I told them was the French equivalent of my name of Italian origin. They had me help with various household and field chores. They took me on a sleigh to Sunday mass, an endless service partly in Breton and partly in Latin. Then we went home for a chicken dinner, the only meal with meat we had all week.

When I returned to Quimper, I discovered the same nervous and somber atmosphere I had sometimes forgotten in the country, where I was completely cut off from the world, since there was no radio or newspaper. Things were complicated: my father was very indecisive by nature; my mother constantly changed her mind, but once she had an idea, she would not rest until she saw it through. One day she wanted to return to Paris; the next she wanted to stay in Brittany. The general mood was atrocious. A bitter discussion with Monsieur Perrault about the incident at Mers el-Kébir put our friendship at risk. The base at Mers el-Kébir, near Oran, sheltered a large number of French battleships at the time of the armistice. The armistice agreements stipulated that the ships in the fleet be disarmed in their port of registry, and the Reich solemnly vowed not to use them for the duration of the war. The French admirals, very legalistic for the most part, wanted to take the German generals at their word, but the English, more clairvoyant and pragmatic, gave no credit to those "scraps of paper" (an expression Hitler himself used to express what he thought of treaties). In addition, the English urgently needed as many battleships as possible to defend their island, and they had no intention of letting the French fleet fall into German hands. It is important to remember that at that time the English were facing the troops of the Third Reich *alone*. Neither the Russians nor the United States had yet entered the war.

On July 3 the English admiral gave an ultimatum to the French admiral, who rejected it and prepared to fight. The English sank the cruiser *Bretagne* and then the *Dunkirk*, killing 1,297 French sailors. In France, as could be expected, the German-controlled radio played upon the patriotic sentiment of the French population, which had just lost two of the jewels of their fleet. Several days after my return from Elliant, we listened to the venomous statements spouting from the radio in the Perraults' living room. I was overcome with anger and declared that the French admiral was stupid, that he was responsible for the loss of the cruisers and the men, that the only thing he could do would be to side with the English and continue fighting the Nazis. Monsieur Perrault, also hotheaded, answered sharply that the English had always been enemies of the French and they had no place giving orders to a French admiral, that I had no idea what went into building those ships and, besides, I couldn't understand the incident because I was "not French"! Hearing those words at such a moment from our oldest, dearest friend was like being burned with a hot poker. I started yelling and declared I was leaving his house forever, that I would never see him again in all my life. Then I went and cried on my bed until I could cry no more.

That episode remains etched in my memory as one of the most important events of my life. A man I cared about deeply thought the cause of a political disagreement was my not being rooted in French soil like him, and that I had no right to speak; this revealed a latent xenophobia that surfaced from the depths to destroy years of friendship in one fell swoop. Despite the excuses he hastened to make, I could not forgive him. The matter was too serious. He had labeled me in such a way as to forbid me from judging current events. At that time, when Jews were faced with the constant threat of being treated as vermin and eliminated by gassing, he had denied me the status of being French, robbing me of the only solid identity I claimed. I had heard our death knell as ostracized Jews in a country that had once welcomed us warmly.

I learned very late, when I was ten, that I had a special identity, through an insult someone spat at me on the playground at Lycée Molière. I went home and asked my mother what a "dirty Jew" was, what it meant to be Jewish.

I no longer remember her surely muddled answer; my mother had been caught in her own trap. Indeed, my parents believed with all their heart that in France they could finally be "like everybody else," with nothing to make them different or mark them as victims in terms of power. Having to explain to me the meaning of the insult I had just suffered extinguished this hope. They didn't know how to tell me the *truth* about the situation that had ruled their past and was determining our future. Their refusal to explain the issue stemmed from their ardent desire to turn their backs on their past life—Austrian, Russian, Polish, always mistrusted, always hunted down—in order to establish a new and finally dignified existence.

It is important to note that my parents were absolutely unreligious, undoubtedly atheist. During their youth in Poland they had been active in groups of Jewish socialists, and they felt only mistrust toward synagogues and rabbis. In France I had no contact with traditional Judaism, except when I visited my grandmothers. I tried to communicate in Polish with my paternal grandmother. In her home I had seen the Sabbath preparations—the pretty candles on the fireplace mantel—but being a child, I never asked questions and didn't know the significance of this ritual. My other grandmother (also the grandmother of Georges Perec) kept a tiny delicatessen in Belleville. I saw her rarely, always in her store, where they spoke only Yiddish and I understood nothing. I went to a synagogue maybe twice in my entire childhood, for the marriages of my aunts. For these reasons, the status of being Jewish had only an external, almost foreign, significance for me. In accordance with my education, I believed I was indistinguishable from the other children.

This explains my violent reaction to Monsieur Perrault: since I attributed no clear meaning to the Jewish identity imposed on me externally, his refusal to recognize me as French stripped me of what I considered my true roots, leaving me bare and defenseless before the Nazis.

Since we couldn't escape the Germans, whether they were in Quimper or Paris, we sadly but sensibly decided to return home toward the end of July. My father wanted to get back to his business, and I wanted to see the Beaver again.

The Beaver was ambivalent: she wanted to see me but was also annoyed, she wrote to Sartre, by my "determinedly desperate reactions," which explains why she said she felt "as indifferent to [Bianca] as ever. To be precise, I no longer find the least thing interesting about her in any respect."[31]

In writing *The Prime of Life* twenty years later using her diaries from 1940, she describes her feelings much more nobly:

> *Bianca was in a state of extreme anxiety and depression, and despite all my efforts to comfort her, I could sense her feeling of complete isolation, even when she was with me. I remembered how once I had said to Olga that there was no such thing as "a Jew," there were only human beings: how head-in-the-clouds I had been! Much earlier in 1939, when Bianca had talked to me about her Viennese cousins, I had foreseen, with a twinge of private shame, that her life was destined to be very different from mine. There was no getting away from the truth of that premonition now. She was in positive danger, whereas I had nothing specific to*

> *fear: neither friendship nor affinity could succeed in bridging the gulf that yawned between us. Neither of us measured the size of that gulf, and her generous nature shied away from plumbing its depths even more than I did. But though she allowed herself no bitterness, I could not escape an uncomfortable feeling very much akin to remorse."*[32]

Her refusal to accept this uncomfortable feeling—ever since she had decided once and for all to be happy—explains in part why she later rejected me. The precarious situation of the Jews—indeed, my own existence—threatened her happiness.

There is perhaps another reason for the difference in tone between the *Letters* and *The Prime of Life*. When she addresses Sartre directly, she doctors things, misrepresents situations, especially those involving me. She adds details, wants to amuse him, to spark his interest. For his benefit she creates vulgar images or caricatures, versions larger than life. Bear in mind that Sartre had broken up with me in February. It was only natural that she paint her partner a sorry picture of me in order to boost his ego. Sartre cast me out of his life because I had lost most of the value I had had in his eyes. Then the Beaver herself got ready to break with me, at the moment I needed her most.

On August 31, because all of my friends had returned from their respective hideouts, we all decided to have a big party. Jacques Besse, an excellent musician who was a former student of Sartre's and classmate of Bernard's, was alone in his parents' large apartment in Neuilly. It was agreed that each of us would bring whatever food he or she could scrounge, for we were just beginning to feel the effects of the shortage. Jacques, the son and grandson of winemakers, would provide the wine and brandy. The party lasted one whole day and half of the next: we ate, drank, sang. Jacques played classical music and jazz for us, and a young actress recited Racine. At nightfall we had no desire to leave, so we slept on the floor and the couches. All my friends drank quite a bit, except me, since alcohol makes me sleepy. Since we had no record player, Bernard offered to get his in the afternoon of the first day. I went with him. It was during that trip that he first kissed me, emboldened by the wine. I must say, that kiss really touched me. It was an invitation to simple pleasure with a boy my own age, a welcome change from my complicated and painful relationships with Sartre and the Beaver. Bernard was attractive, quite handsome, with a wide forehead and a face that made him look a bit like the poet Paul Éluard. His smile was sometimes kind, sometimes sarcastic. He had a good sense of humor, often black humor that expressed his pessimism. His first passion was poetry; later he became fascinated with dada and surrealism (he wrote his own surrealist poems). But what changed his entire life was his discovery of jazz, which he knew like the back of his hand. He was completely immersed in it, which created a closeness between him and Jacques Besse. Known for his discretion, he spoke little of his passions. He was very reserved, shy, almost secretive, and his mysterious silence was sometimes rather frightening. Sartre's teachings had steered him toward philosophy; it wasn't until much later that I realized he was interested as much in the arts and in literature as in abstract theories. He nevertheless studied hard at the university, because of the solid training he had received from the Jesuits at Collège Saint-Joseph in Lille, and most of all because he wanted a stable source of income.

Toward the end of September, I invited the Beaver on a real bike trip with me, since biking seemed to be her latest passion. We decided to visit the Morbihan. We got off the train before Nantes, wandered around Guérande, crossed the wilderness of La Baule, and then methodically toured the entire department. We kept a swift pace, traveling about a hundred kilometers per day, stopping in villages and visiting churches and châteaux. We were in good shape. I had always bicycled a lot; the Beaver had calves of steel and was very eager to see everything. We discovered that biking was a wonderful way to get to know a country—you could see the scenery better than from a car, while traveling faster than on foot. In any case, we had a lot of fun and got along well, as we had before. Sometimes the ride was particularly hard, as when we had to go up the Quiberon Peninsula with a headwind. This athletic camaraderie probably kept me from detecting the chill in the Beaver's feelings. After admiring Rochefort-en-Terre, we returned to Paris. In her short account of our ride in Brittany, Simone de Beauvoir concludes, "We met no Germans on the road. . . . During this fortnight I managed to forget them almost completely: a faint flicker of the old peacetime *douceur de vivre* glowed into transient life. Then we returned to Paris."[33]

When we got back, however, I could feel that the Beaver was distancing herself from me. Maybe she considered our ride a good-bye trip. I didn't know that Jacques-Laurent Bost (Little Bost) was there and that she was growing more and more fond of him. He had been wounded in combat in

1940 and was finishing his convalescence. She informed me she could no longer see me as much as before, that we had to cut down on the amount of time we spent together. Since I protested vigorously and desperately, she finally confessed she was having an "idyll" (that's the expression she used) with Bost. Suddenly I was suffocating, sinking. I resisted as much as I could. I figured out that this idyll was nothing new and reproached her forcefully for having lied to me. She told me she had been reluctant to tell me about it for fear of hurting me. This lie only deepened my sorrow, for I couldn't stand anyone lying to me about something so important. I felt abandoned, humiliated for the second time in a year, torn apart, deserted. The entire marvelous adventure, that attractive three-part structure, collapsed like a house of cards. I was desperate beyond words, because my attachment to the Beaver had been much deeper than my feelings toward Sartre.

As I remember it, and my memory is very clear regarding this incident, I was the one who decided to immediately sever all ties with her. I couldn't stand halfhearted efforts; I didn't want to be attached to her, since she wanted nothing to do with me. But perhaps I changed my mind about that sudden decision, since Simone de Beauvoir mentions in her letters (if she is telling the truth) that we saw each other several times, less and less frequently, until I got married.

The Beaver easily accepted how much she hurt others. In her letter to Sartre dated October 18, she describes the situation as follows: "I've more or less broken with Bianca. There were tears (I told her all about Bost), but she's having an idyll with Ramblin [Lamblin], so that's working out."[34] Thus, it reassured her that I had started to become interested in Bernard. She believed that one feeling could replace another, like pieces on a chessboard. She gave no thought to how deeply I had been hurt. After she had grown tired of me, gotten Sartre to break with me first, become more interested than ever in her relationship with Little Bost (on the day we broke up, she confessed that she had discovered she preferred sex with men to sex with women), why bother? To hell with vows and promises of life as a threesome!

Now the triangle was completely shattered. I had been pathetically cast off, and that double execution took place in 1940. Although it was on a more personal level, this deliberate attempt to destroy me came at the same time as the collapse of the country under the weight of Hitler's army and the abject submission of French authorities to Nazi laws. Now that so many years have passed since the wound was inflicted, I can say that despite appearances, despite my ability to "bounce back" and rebuild my life, I have carried the weight of that abandonment my entire life. The only way I can describe how I felt then is to use the image of a drowning person who grabs hold of a log and manages miraculously to survive. Similarly, despite my genuine despair, I clung instinctively to life and managed not to hit rock bottom.

Indeed, it might appear as if I was on the road to recovery, since I had become involved in a new romantic relationship even before our separation. Simone de Beauvoir's letters to Sartre allude to this several times: she writes that she is surprised at my growing interest in Bernard. Actually, I felt at the same time sorrow for their abandoning me and the awakening of a new love.

The War

Having described my personal feelings, I shall now focus on collective experiences. On October 2, 1940, a German order enjoined all Jews to declare themselves, all Jewish businesses to make themselves known. After numerous discussions and much hesitation, my father—like almost all the Jews I knew—went to the commissariat to register.[35] He was afraid that if he did not declare himself he would be accused of wrongdoing, and he didn't know what the consequences would be. Actually, it would have been better had he not declared himself, but with a name like David Bienenfeld he was right to fear the authorities. At the same time, he initiated various procedures to leave for the United States, but for unknown reasons none of his efforts were successful. Then he conceived of a special rescue for me: he had learned that by marrying a U.S. citizen, you could go to America with him or her. Once you got there, all you had to do was annul this marriage of convenience by getting a divorce. He suggested this "scheme" to me, but I was not at all interested. First of all, I would have had to leave Bernard, with whom I was in love. Second, I would have had to leave my parents and sister alone to face the mortal dangers of the German occupation. Finally, getting married in this way would have thrown me into an uncertain, unpleasant situation. But my father, who saw clearly the dangers we all faced, insisted vehemently that I accept. Reluctantly, I gave in. Who knows how, Father found a young American living in Montparnasse. First he gave the young man money, then he bought him a suit. The Sixteenth Arrondissement city hall published a marriage announcement;

witnesses were called in. On the scheduled day, we all went to the city hall. The American didn't show up, and we never saw him again. We learned later that he had drunk himself silly with my father's money, and he was sleeping at the time set for the ceremony. All that effort for nothing. I called Bernard, happy to tell him the news. In a vague sort of way, I probably wanted my fate to match the common fate, that of my family. Furthermore, the most important thing for me was to stay near Bernard—this desire erased my fear of danger.

The Beaver, it appears from reading *Letters to Sartre*, was cold and completely indifferent to whatever problems I might have been having. After noting that "it seems that my break with Bianca is definitive, and I no longer hear anything of her," she writes, "I went off to take the Métro and meet Bianca at Le Passy, in order to go with her to the Conservatoire rehearsal. As I've told you, we broke off, then made up again—and it's just limping along. But we're dragging it out, because she's going to be married in a fortnight and follow her husband to America. We probably shan't ever see each other again, and that solves the problem. Ramblin's in despair as usual." In her letter dated December 31, her tone becomes downright venomous: "I spotted Bienenfeld—who now permanently has quivering nostrils, difficulty in breathing, and anguish of spirit. Her father was conferring with M. Ramblin: she knows she's getting married in a fortnight, but doesn't know to whom—Ramblin or the American? It's a pitiful situation, yet one with which I can summon up no sympathy."[36]

Her absolutely uncalled-for cruelty and refusal to appreciate the turmoil of most Jews living in the occupied zone was probably caused in part by sheer frustration. She was the one who threw me out of her life, but when she learned that I was trying to move on, that I had fallen in love with one of my classmates, she became bitter about it. There is no other way to explain why she confused the marriage of convenience, destined only to get me out of France, with my plans to marry Bernard, based on love and friendship and entirely different motives. But added to her frustration was the irritation she always felt regarding marriage, which she automatically associated with bourgeois life and viewed as ridiculous and odious. As if only the bourgeois married and had children!

After that failed effort to get me to the United States, my parents encouraged me to marry Bernard. They were always worried about what could happen to me and saw my growing attachment to him. Marrying him would give me the protection of a French-sounding name, which would perhaps be helpful if I were ever confronted by the authorities. It was their idea, not mine: one morning, they asked me, "Would you like to marry Bernard?" At first, I found this question strange. Indeed, in those days people didn't marry until they were able to support themselves. Normally, we would have had to complete our studies and obtain our degrees before considering marriage. But times were not normal: you had to save your skin. The rules of etiquette did not apply. I took my father's words seriously and spoke to Bernard shortly thereafter.

First, I had to tell him about my double affair with Sartre and the Beaver, and of our breakup. The two of us were sitting in the Jardin du Luxembourg; I spoke and Bernard listened without saying a word. When I had finished my story, I did not hide the fact that I was still very upset about my past loves and still reeling from the blow. I told him he also needed to know that marrying me would put his career as a professor at risk, because the Nazis would try to destroy mixed households and persecute men stupid enough to marry Jewish women: that is what the Nazis were doing in Germany. I asked Bernard to reflect on all this before letting me know his decision. His desire to marry me remained unswayed. All we had to do was see his parents, to whom I explained the foreseeable consequences of marrying a Jew. Several days later they told me they were willing for Bernard to marry me in spite of everything, which surprised and deeply touched me, coming from members of the French bourgeoisie. I respected and appreciated them for it. I think that parents such as Bernard's, who could agree to such a marriage for their only son, were rare at that time. It is true that Bernard was deeply in love, and this touched my very romantic mother-in-law. All that my future in-laws asked in return was that we agree to baptize our children. Even though both of us were complete atheists, we promised to do so.

We were married informally on February 12, 1941, at the city hall in the Sixteenth Arrondissement. When we left the restaurant where we celebrated the event, we saw a squad of German soldiers parade by, marching in rhythm to a soldier's chant. An ominous sight. Then we got back to our studies, because we had to obtain certain certificates that had been delayed. It was only after we had passed our exams that we went away to relax in the Basque country. We were exhausted but happy to be together, to walk along the wild beaches and in the hills. However, everything I had just experienced came crashing down on me, and I fell into a true depression. I cried myself to sleep every night. I couldn't stop sobbing, even though I realized how it must have hurt Bernard. But he was so compassionate, so loving and kind that his mere presence comforted me—I saw that I could count on him. I went to a doctor who tried to treat me with injections. That was definitely not a very encouraging beginning to married life. Bernard needed all his innate love and generosity to accept the way things were.

After that month of rest, we returned to Paris and moved into a small apartment my mother had rented and partially furnished for us on Rue Vésale near Carrefour des Gobelins. In March we learned that Sartre had returned, having managed to be freed from his prison camp by means of a fake medical certificate.[37] Of course, we had broken all ties with him and Simone de Beauvoir, but we sometimes got news of them through Raoul Lévy, who still saw them. Our friends told us of the creation of Socialism and Freedom, a pseudo-resistance group, but what they told us only drove us away. Pretentiousness, irresponsibility, ineffectiveness—the "action" of Sartre and his entourage was revolting. We were worried that imprudence and carelessness would get one of our friends into trouble. Luckily, nothing of the sort happened. Yvonne Picard's arrest in June 1942 had nothing to do with the activities of Socialism and Freedom: Yvonne, whom we liked a great deal, had realized how amateurish that group was and left some time before to join the Communist Youth Movement. Sartre had once taken it upon himself to write the future constitution of the state of France! That text truly existed. Raoul often spoke of it to us, and together we poked fun at the pretentiousness of its author, who apparently shrank from nothing. It's too bad that text has apparently been lost: we could have read one of the most important provisions of the future constitution, stipulating that professors who are also writers be given paid leave!

At first, the Occupation was the same for us as for most French people: a search for food and warmth and a constant vigilance to try to escape arrest. Our apartment was freezing cold, and it was very hard to live there during the harsh winter of 1941–42. We often worked in libraries or cafés, and in desperation we went to the greenhouse at the Jardin des Plantes, where it was delightfully warm and lovely. We were saved from undernourishment by the packages of potatoes, lard, and eggs Madame Lennon sent us from the farm. A certain number of other Parisians were in the same boat: their families or friends in the country supplied them with food. During the 1941–42 academic year, Professor Jean Wahl was dismissed from his chair at the Sorbonne. Emile Bréhier notified him of that administrative decision, for which Wahl never forgave him. Furious not to be able to practice his profession, he decided to continue teaching in the salon of his hotel, on Rue des Beaux-Arts. Several of his students, including Bernard and me, went every week to hear the master and have discussions with him. We were all unaware of the risk we ran. Jean Wahl seemed to live in another world, far away from the threats that already plagued us all. Regardless, he was arrested and sent to Drancy. Luckily, he managed to be freed and left for the United States. As for me, apart from this exposure to philosophy that stemmed more from loyalty and friendship than from genuine interest in pure thought, I remained far removed from abstract problems and could maintain interest only in events related to the war. It is important to understand that we were at rock bottom, having no idea whatsoever how the war would turn out. Not until February 1943 and the end of the siege of Stalingrad, which had been surrounded since October 1942, could we begin to see a light at the end of the tunnel.

My father wanted to stay in Paris, where he managed to do some business. He guessed that very soon he would need money to support his family, because in that time of persecution money was vital. My mother was very distressed and encouraged my father to leave Paris. The decree of March 21, 1941, was especially dangerous, as it revoked French nationality from my entire family (including me). We became stateless persons, first in line for arrest and deporta-

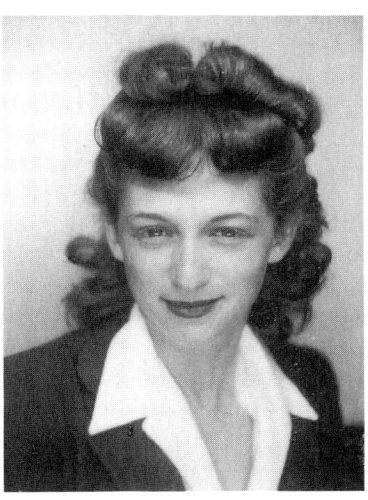

Bianca Bienenfeld in 1941, at the age of twenty.

tion. Because I was married to a true French citizen, I alone regained my French nationality by a corrected decree in July.

Only after he miraculously escaped arrest in June 1941 did my father finally agree to leave. There was an I.D. check at the Cadet Metro station, where my father got off every day to go to his office. The police questioned all the passengers, examined their papers, and picked up everyone who looked Jewish. Luckily, my father had gotten off at the preceding station that day, in order to meet a friend. That time he was truly frightened and resigned himself to leaving his business. He left for Villard-de-Lans with my mother and sister, to join one of my aunts who was already living there.

Bernard and I were left alone in Paris, almost—Bernard's parents were still living in Neuilly, and my maternal grandparents and Aunt Cécile, Georges Perec's mother, lived meagerly in Belleville. My grandmother still had her tiny Jewish delicatessen there, and my grandfather mumbled into his beard on the way to synagogue and spoke Yiddish with his friends, as usual. Cécile had been forced to give up her job as a hairstylist for lack of clients and now worked at the Jaz factory in Suresnes. Once settled in Villard-de-Lans, my mother told her sister-in-law she could send little Georges to the mountains, where my mother could take care of him. My mother was very attached to Georges, whose father—her little brother—she had often cared for. My aunt hesitated for quite a while; she was deeply scarred by the death of her husband, a volunteer in a foreign regiment, killed in action several days before the armistice. It was impossible for her to fathom being separated from her son. Finally she accepted, for the child's sake: the threats, especially in that quarter of Belleville, were becoming more and more serious. One November evening in 1941, Cécile and I drove Georges to the Gare de Lyon. He was five and a half years old and wasn't fully aware of what was happening. His mother had bought him a *Charlot* magazine, which he mentions in *W, or The Memory of Childhood*.[38] Around his neck he wore a sign with his name and destination. The women in the Red Cross escorted such children, in principle all "sons of war veterans." My mother was to meet Georges at the end of the trip, in Grenoble, and take him into her care.

Lonely without her son and very depressed by his departure, Cécile often came to see us on the weekends. She sometimes brought us a piece of meat she had bought on the black market. We would discuss Georges, about whom we had received good news, and talk about her life and the very difficult conditions she faced. She would get up at five o'clock every morning, take the Metro and the train from Belleville to Suresnes, and work nine hours. She was in constant danger of being questioned en route and especially of getting caught in a police raid in Belleville itself. More than once, we advised her to find herself a little room in Suresnes. With her war widow's card in the name of Cécile Perec, she would have been safe. But Cécile was a shy, gentle woman who needed to go home to her family in Belleville every evening. She refused to listen to us. Cécile (Cyrla Perec) was arrested on January 23, 1943, sent to Drancy, and deported to Auschwitz on train 47 on February 11. My grandfather was arrested on February 11, 1943, and left Drancy on March 2 on train 49. From what my mother could gather later, he never made it to Auschwitz: old and frail, he apparently died in the sealed car that carried him away. Grandmother, who had been in another part of the city during the raid, had a narrow escape, then hid with friends, and finally left to join my parents. She spent the rest of the war in Lans.

Life during the Occupation inspired all sorts of reactions, from distress, obliviousness, and horror to comedy and ridicule—it was all mixed together. One day, when Bernard and I were walking on the Grands Boulevards, we stopped to look in a shop window when someone tapped Bernard on the shoulder. When we turned around, we found ourselves face to face with Simone Kamenker, a friend of Bernard's, the woman who was later to become Simone Signoret. Seeing I was not wearing a star on my coat (and neither was she!), she cried, "You really shouldn't walk around like that! It's very dangerous, very risky!" We motioned for her to be quiet and quickly took flight. Had a militiaman, a simple informer (of which there were plenty at that time), or a zealous German been nearby, I would probably have finished my life in a camp.

My relationship with Bernard had completely changed. For one thing, my sorrow had lessened. Everyday worries and the somber outlook for the future absorbed us. In addition, Bernard came down more and more often from his poetic cloud in order to be with me. Indeed, in the early days of our marriage, what disconcerted me most was the way he would sometimes enclose himself in a bubble as invisible as it was impenetrable. In such a state, he could drift along in surrealist style for hours, never deigning to answer my questions or react to my exasperation. In this manner, he would break all lines of communication, or maybe he refused to accept the platitudes of everyday existence and needed to protect himself from married life. I felt more than forgotten, erased, denied. However, these episodes became less and less frequent.

We were linked by true love and unreserved respect. Our relationship was based on constant mutual seduction. We discovered love through various games: while it's true we had a lot to learn, our youth and sensuality made up for our ignorance and brought us closer together. The permanent danger in which we lived added a feeling of urgency, encouraged us to live without delay. Besides philosophy, we shared all sorts of common interests: literature, painting, music. Bernard was much more cultivated than I in certain areas. In addition to his traditional education and study of philosophy, he was a true self-taught man. He had discovered poetry during his sad, lonely childhood, devouring Racine at the age of ten. By listening to the famous tunes played on cinema organs, he discovered jazz during intermissions in the suburban auditoriums where he would go on Thursdays with his friends. That was when he began to explore the vast domain of that new music with a lively rhythm and sense of imagination that especially attracted him. He knew *everything* about the bands, major musicians, and jam sessions. He explained to me the structure of jazz; he played for me and helped me to recognize the sounds of different instruments, to appreciate the "swing," that lilt that gives it life. It was a true passion. Until then, I had known only classical music, piano, symphony orchestra. That was the music that I, in turn, tried to help Bernard understand. He didn't appreciate it until much later, however, when he heard *The Firebird*. Starting with Stravinsky, he discovered symphonic music and later opera.

We also loved art. Together we went to shows at the Galerie Carré and other places on Avenue de Messine and Rue la Boétie. That was the artistic heart of Paris. There we admired Jacques Villon, Rouault, Vieira da Silva, and many others. Our friend Claude Simonnet, brother-in-law of Alfred Manessier, introduced us to the world of the *nouvelle peinture* artists. Manessier lived in the country, and he let Claude live in a little house with a studio on the top floor, at the end of a courtyard on Rue de Vaugirard. That was his home in Paris. We often had friendly gatherings there in the evenings, with Raoul Lévy, Jean Kanapa, Claudine Retail, and Yvonne Picard. Our friendship with Alfred Manessier and his wife has lasted through thick and thin. Through him we were exposed to the whole "lyrical abstraction" movement that was about be born in France.

I still had bitter memories of the "threesome" that had hurt me, even though I was full of hope about beginning a new life with Bernard. In a drawer I had stashed the packet of letters, *all* my letters from Sartre. One evening toward the end of the winter of 1942, we were invited to dinner by our friends the Simonnets. I took the packet with me and asked them if I could throw it into their furnace. I thus burned perhaps forty letters, feeling as though I was accomplishing an act of justice and eliminating the traces of my odious past.

The following spring, the French authorities, by order of the Germans, required Jews to have the word "Jew" stamped in red on their I.D. cards. In addition, each person was given three yellow fabric stars printed with the word "Jew" in Gothic letters. These were to be sewn onto clothing so as to be visible. I went to the commissariat to go through these formalities, but once I got home I buried the stars at the bottom of a drawer and never wore them (I saved them as evidence of the brand they tried to inflict on me). Of course, I risked arrest. But it made no difference: owing to the simple fact that I was Jewish, that risk hovered over me constantly anyway.

A little later, at the end of spring, the concierge notified us that a police officer had come looking for me and left a summons. Had there been an informer? Was there merely an administrative question? In general, that was not how people were arrested. I did not respond to the summons, and I never heard what happened, but we heeded the warning: we prepared to leave Paris and join my parents in Villard-de-Lans.

It was the beginning of the summer of 1942. Yvonne Picard had been arrested on June 18 under scandalous conditions and was in jail. All her friends were extremely upset.[39] The threats of General von Stülpnagel, the prisoner executions, the showing of *The Jew against France* followed by *Bolshevism against Europe*, the opening of the case of Riom, and so many other sinister omens convinced us it was high time to head for the free zone.

Bernard had no problem simply taking the train, since he was a French student. For me, things were much more dangerous. I needed to find someone to smuggle me through. Raoul Lévy's father was the one who suggested I ask the deputy of the Nièvre, whose name I do not recall.

According to our arrangement, he was to take me with him by train as far as Nevers. From there he promised me an easy passage by car across the border. I paid him a large sum of money in advance and took the train with him. Upon arriving in Nevers, he left me in a little hotel, telling me a smuggler would come for me in the evening. The border zone was under heavy surveillance by the German army; I was risking my life. I waited in vain, tortured by fear. I had with me only my official family record book, having judiciously decided to leave behind my I.D. card stamped with the word "Jew." The hotel had no vacant rooms, so I slept on an armchair, grateful they hadn't turned me away. The next morning, in a rage, I went to the hotel where the deputy lived and started yelling and screaming. Finally, seized with fear, he came outside and tried to calm me down. He swore that that very evening someone would come for me. A man finally arrived and drove me to the gathering point. There I realized that at least a dozen people, most of them Jewish, were participating in the operation. Some were elderly women who had trouble walking and couldn't stay quiet—they kept moaning loudly, putting us all in danger. I was furious. What was happening was not at all what the deputy had promised. Night fell. For some time we advanced slowly along a road. Finally, we were led into a field and told to be as quiet as possible, because the little road nearby, which was also the border, was constantly patrolled by Germans. The smuggler went off to survey the area. We waited a long time, intrigued and extremely worried by strange noises that sounded almost like footsteps. Finally, we noticed the outline of several cows in the darkness: we had mistaken their steady rumination for the crackling of heavy boots. The smuggler came back and hurried us across the road. Then we tumbled down an embankment to the Nièvre, where a boat took us to the other side. At last we were in the free zone!

But we were not free. We slept a few hours at an inn, all crammed together. We awoke to a very unpleasant surprise: the police were waiting downstairs to interrogate us. What rotten luck! When it was my turn, I showed them my family record book, in which it was written that I was born in Lublin in April 1921. I thought my father's and mother's names would sound so strange to the French policeman that all was lost. He asked, "Are you a Jew?" I quickly and vehemently answered no and explained that my father, of Alsatian origin, was a diplomat, and I had been born in Poland on one of his missions. He wavered a split second, then returned my book. During that moment, my life had hung in the balance between his duty and his compassion. He knew full well that I was Jewish, but my lie was the pretext he needed to turn his back—otherwise I would have been sent to prison, then to a camp like Gurs, and finally handed over to the German authorities of the occupied zone.

That was a narrow escape. I was both distressed and happy when I called Villard. I was reunited with my parents and Bernard, who awaited me anxiously. We could finally breathe a sigh of relief. After several weeks' rest, we decided to settle in Aix-en-Provence, because Bernard wanted to continue his studies and prepare for his degree. He was thrilled to be able to work under Gaston Berger. Raoul Lévy joined us again, and the three of us began spending a lot of time together, which was quite pleasant at first. We got back in touch with Pierrot Guastalla and his family, whom we loved dearly. Pierrot was as exuberant and cheerful as ever. He knew many people in Aix and was often invited to the "Château Noir," where the painter Tal Coat hosted simple, interesting gatherings. But I didn't participate in those social events. I was withdrawn, very depressed, dried up—I just wasn't myself. I wanted nothing and couldn't enjoy that delightful city the way my friends did, strolling around day and night in the courtyards and squares with gushing fountains. One day, when Pierrot and I were eating lunch in the restaurant at the Hôtel du Roi René, I took a slice of ham out of my purse to spice up the ground "spinach" (which was really just grass). I did not offer any to Pierrot. He was so good and so thoughtful that he forgave me that petty act, because he was aware of what I had been through and knew I still felt miserable. Indeed, when we had become friends in Rennes, he had rather indiscreetly read my little personal notebook in which I wrote down my thoughts each day. When he returned it, he asked me some questions, and we discussed at length my experiences with Sartre and the Beaver. In Aix, Pierrot forgave me, but I have never been able to forgive my own stinginess. That incident showed me just how severely my personality had deteriorated.

On November 11, 1942, "History with a capital H," in the words of Georges Perec, caught up with us. The Allied landing in northern Africa gave the Germans a good excuse to invade all of France. No more line of demarcation, no more supposed free zone. All the pretenses that had made the collaborators feel smug collapsed at the same time: the country faced the harsh reality of occupation.

Bernard, Raoul, and I had only two months of relative

peace in Aix. Then the city started to buzz with crazy rumors. Panic overcame even the calmest spirits. Those who have not experienced war must understand that this turmoil was neither gratuitous nor comical but real, caused by a perfectly valid fear: many Jews of the occupied zone had sought refuge in the nonoccupied zone (*zone non occupée* or "nono"). There they had led a sometimes precarious existence but were relatively safe. Now the line of demarcation that was supposed to protect them was suddenly erased, leaving them defenseless against the Nazis and their henchmen, the Darnand militia. Our neighbor Monsieur Verboeckhaven, a Jew of Belgian origin who lived on the top floor of the villa where we occupied the ground floor, combed the city on his racing bike and returned with his pouch full of false (or true) news, each item more alarming than the one before. He thoroughly unnerved us.

The Italian army was occupying the area around Grenoble (including Villard-de-Lans). There was a significant difference between the Italian and German occupation. Indeed, the Italian army had no particular animosity toward the French population nor toward the Jews. For about a year, that area of France was therefore a sort of haven compared to the rest of the country. But in July 1943 Mussolini was overthrown, and in August Italy surrendered unconditionally. German soldiers replaced the Italians. My father's entire family, as well as my father himself, my mother, and my sister, obtained false papers and moved—some to La Chapelle-en-Vercors and some to Saint-Martin. My father's name became Monsieur Blanchard and my mother's Madame Beauchamp, but since Mother was more popular in town than Father, the residents of Saint-Martin soon began calling my father Monsieur Beauchamp!

When my parents left Villard for Saint-Martin-en-Vercors, they left little Georges Perec at the church, under the watchful care of the headmistress, a woman of admirable courage and devotion. My parents paid several months' boarding fees to ensure their nephew's safety, whatever might happen to them. My maternal grandmother was staying in a small room in Lans. My parents helped her financially, but she was very independent by nature and wanted to live alone. Although she had great difficulty because she barely spoke French, she managed to get a job as a cook at a children's boarding house. We found her in good health after the Liberation. After the war, she didn't want to remain in France: she joined Léon, her second son, in Israel, where he had settled in 1934. She died there at an advanced age.

~~~

After German troops had occupied the entire free zone, Bernard, Raoul, and I were forced to obtain false papers. For Raoul and me, the reasons were obvious. For Bernard, it was a matter of protecting himself from the law establishing forced labor (*le service de travail obligatoire*, or STO). This law, put into force on September 4, 1942, stipulated that "all men eighteen to fifty years old and all single women twenty-one to thirty-five be called up in order to perform such labor as the government [deemed] useful, in the higher interest of the nation" (meaning the Germans). This law, slow to be applied, was not enough for Fritz Sauckel, head of labor recruiting. He needed workers fast. On February 16, 1943, Laval therefore called up all men born between January 1, 1920, and December 31, 1922. The forced-labor law became a real threat. Bernard and Raoul were afraid of being sent to Germany to work in factories that were constantly being bombed. In addition, they didn't want to contribute to the Reich's war effort. The three of us therefore had to have fake I.D. cards made. We arranged for these fake cards to look "real" (we knew what a "real-fake passport" was!) and not cost anything. To look real, they had to be registered in a city hall. We went to Montpellier, home of our friend Rolland Caillois, to register them. One evening in Aix, Bernard—ever meticulous and wary—was examining my card. He cried out in horror, seeing that I had automatically signed "B. Lamblin." Feeling sheepish about my careless mistake, I did what I could to alter the signature.

One day not long afterward, I was strolling along Rue Mirabeau with Pierrot Guastalla when he said to me, "I have to say good-bye. I'm taking a bus to Spain in fifteen minutes, and I'm going to try to get to northern Africa to enlist. I can't stand it anymore—being here and doing nothing. So, good luck to you!" He embraced me warmly. I was speechless, extremely upset. With Pierrot leaving, I was losing a very good friend, a loyal, intelligent, and loving friend. I was also torn apart because he had told me nothing about his decision until that day, which meant he did not trust me completely. The bus was waiting. In tears, I embraced him. I didn't know at the time that I was never to see him again. Despite many difficulties and months in prison in Spain, he finally reached Algeria and managed to enlist in General Leclerc's army. In 1944 his regiment, integrated into the Second Armored Division, landed in Normandy and advanced toward Paris. Pierrot was killed near Bourget in a burst of gunfire while on patrol as a volunteer. When I returned to Paris from Grenoble in September 1944, I did not know he was dead. On the contrary, I found a note—a few friendly and cheerful words—he had scribbled in haste and left with my concierge. His mother, Lina, was the one who told me he was dead. She was quite shaken, but her sadness was calm and deep, as she was. I continued to visit her regularly, for Pierrot had loved her more than anything and I also cherished her. A bit later, she had some of her son's writings published, in particular his *Journal*. In a moment of foresight he had written in his diary, "I am obsessed with the passage of time and people who die without creating anything."[40] His life, cut short by the war he faced with courage, ended before he could truly develop any important work.

While I think of Pierrot with affection and admiration, I contrast his qualities with my own attitude during that period when so many people devoted themselves in so many ways to the Resistance or to the army, as he did. My passivity, my lack of any sort of commitment, demands an explanation. Pierrot was too aware of my constant depression to think of asking for my help, so he didn't. But a good friend of mine from class, who lived in Marseille and with whom I had regained contact, asked me to work with her resistance group affiliated with the Communist party. I consented, but she could probably tell how reluctant I was: she never sent anyone to see me. As early as the summer of 1942, when I was with my parents in Villard, Doctor Samuel Ravalec, who knew my father well, had strongly urged me not to dwell on my personal failures in that time of war. We had a long talk about it. I knew he was absolutely right.

Everything I believed in should have led me to become active in a network, but I didn't. The force that stopped me was internal: I felt as though my vitality had been totally squelched, as though I had lost all my energy, motivation, and courage. This led to a sort of block, an excessive fear of possible danger and, above all, misgivings about my responsibility toward others. These misgivings paralyzed me. I thought that I would not be a good recruit for a resistance movement and that, given my weakness, I might be a danger to my peers. This explains but does not justify my inaction, a lasting consequence of the psychological collapse of 1940 that left me a wreck, unable to boost myself up.

In May or June, after Bernard had defended his thesis on "Existence in the Philosophy of Berkeley" before Gaston Berger, we decided to return to Paris, where my father-in-law thought he could find a solution more reliable than a mere fake I.D. card to prevent his son from being sent to work in Germany. But it would have been too dangerous to move back to our apartment on Rue Vésale. It had surely been discovered by the police, and there might be an informer living there. We therefore had to look for a furnished apartment. The first place we lived in was on the seventh floor of a building on Rue Daubenton overlooking the mosque. It was a tiny place that was freezing, as we discovered the following winter. Madame Grocholska, the owner of the apartment, asked to see our papers. Bernard held out his card bearing his real name while I showed one with the name Élisabeth Davet. Upon seeing this, Madame Grocholska asked us to tell the other residents we were Monsieur and Madame Lamblin, out of respect for propriety! The fake cards thus continued to get us into some comical situations. My father-in-law had found Bernard a pseudo-job as a blue-collar worker in the Gnôme et Rhône factories on Boulevard Kellermann. That was not far from our place at Censier-Daubenton. Bernard bought himself a pair of overalls and a lunch box, which I filled with a bite to eat when I could, so he wouldn't have to use the pathetic cafeteria at the factory too often. He had to be there nine hours a day. His "job" consisted of filling in equipment receipt slips and carrying various papers from office to office. Nothing too tiring.

Meanwhile, I moped around the studio on Rue Daubenton and spent most of my time standing in endless lines to get a bit of food. Then, in the nearly blinding light of that lofty little room, I would pull an old down comforter up to my chin, making me look as if I really was inside a cocoon. I would put on mittens and try to read some philosophy. But what interested me more than anything else was the English radio, which I listened to with the volume turned low, since next to my room lived a young woman who worked at the Kommandatur. As soon as I heard her come home, I would turn off the radio. The days seemed very long. None of our friends were in Paris—in any case, I don't remember seeing any of them. Nor did I try to get in touch with Simone de Beauvoir; I had no desire whatsoever to see her again under the circumstances in which we lived. In addition, since I was using a false name, I feared the indiscretions of her milieu, whose carelessness I had already experienced.

I did learn something during that stay near the mosque: the best way to hide is not to run to the forest or burrow into a cave, but to live under a false name, three streets away from your former residence. I never ran into anyone who lived in the building on Rue Vésale. And we were careful never to go there.

Later, we moved into a little furnished hotel on Rue des Feuillantines, where we had more space. That hotel was so filthy and dingy that one night we awoke to find bedbugs on the sheet. We insisted the landlord send for the city health department, who disinfected our two-room apartment. Toward the middle of February, I noticed that Bernard's face had turned yellow; he had contracted viral hepatitis, then simply called jaundice. He needed ample rest and a strict diet. My parents-in-law offered to let us stay with them, since they could properly care for their son. When his sick leave came to an end, he had to think about going back to work. It was March 1944. From his workmates, Bernard learned that Germans were planning to transplant the entire factory—both personnel and equipment—to the Hamburg region, a target of heavy bombing by the American flying fortresses. Our decision was made: we would join my parents in the Vercors.

We arrived in Saint-Martin at the beginning of April. At first, we felt relieved to be far away from the German patrols and French police. We could almost feel the freedom in our bones and were enchanted with the blue sky, the fields, the fresh, light air. We rented a room from the Lattard sisters, haberdashers, across from the church. My parents and sister lived several houses down, on Route des Barraques, at Madame Guérin's. Soon, we realized that peace was only an illusion frequently shattered by raids by the militia or the

Germans, who generally acted on orders. If the Germans found a *maquisard*[41] alone on a farm, or a small group of draft dodgers in the mountains, they would gun down the poor people on the spot without any sort of trial. "Terrorists! Terrorists!" the German soldiers would cry. Farmers who had given these people shelter were also killed and their farms burned. We discovered that the war was there all right, but in a form different from what we had known in the city. What was different was that the population was spread out, but everybody knew still each other. The horrors perpetrated in the city were more anonymous, generally involving people we didn't know, and more quickly forgotten.

One week after our arrival, we heard heavy footsteps in our stairway. The door was kicked open suddenly, and two militiamen with machine guns ordered Bernard to show his papers. Since these papers were in perfect order, including his certificate of convalescence, they grudgingly turned on their heels and left us alone. Still, we were shaken, since their visit meant there was an informer in town who had lost no time in reporting our presence.

We spent April and May in Saint-Martin near my parents and their friends. We were surrounded by courageous and loyal people, all members of the Resistance. Among them were the parish priest and the postman. The postman played a key role, since as soon as a militia car or tracked vehicle belonging to German soldiers began the ascent to the Vercors, either by the gorges of the Bourne or by the Grands Goulets, he was warned immediately by his colleague on the plains through a prearranged signal. The postman then warned everyone who had reason to fear these visits. It was a simple, foolproof system that saved many *maquisards*.

Before describing events as I experienced and understood them, I believe it would be useful to describe how the Vercors was configured. This mountainous area between Grenoble to the north and Die to the south is a sort of natural fortress, accessible only by very steep gorges, except above Grenoble. This explains why the Resistance leaders thought to take advantage of this natural formation, the basis of the "Montagnards" plan. In fact, the authors of this plan had foreseen using the Vercors only in the case of an Allied landing in the south of France. The military committee in charge of the operation included Chavant, Le Ray, Eugène Samuel, Jean Prévost, and Costa de Beauregard. However, dissention among the different movements that made up the Resistance (from communists to career officers), a severe lack of organization in the offices in Algiers (headquarters of General de Gaulle's regiment), and the friction between de Gaulle and the Allies led to the tragedy of the Vercors. It is difficult to determine exactly who caused this drama.

On the morning of June 6, the news we had all been waiting for so impatiently finally broke. We could feel our excitement mounting. A feverish agitation overcame the villages and Maquis groups. Career officers took their uniforms out of the closet and put them on. Some, including Captain Tanant and Commander Huet, decided to set up their headquarters in Saint-Martin, which Clément ("Chavant"), the civilian leader of the plateau with the *Francs-tireurs et partisans français* (FTP), was already using as his center of activities. The villa in which headquarters was set up was about a hundred meters away from my parents' house. Around June 15 Commander Hervieux decided to call for volunteers. Bernard stepped forward; because he had never held a weapon in his life, he was made a telephone operator. He worked with two others to ensure a twenty-four-hour connection between the various outposts of the plateau and beyond. I became the cook at headquarters. I spent my days frying potatoes and grilling steaks for officers as well as enlisted men who returned exhausted from combat to give their reports.

We tried to help settle all the people who poured in from the plains and wanted to fight, but in the beginning there were not enough instructors, nowhere to house the men, and not enough arms, even light weapons. Later, thanks to parachute drops, the shortage eased up, but the officers were concerned about the lack of heavy artillery promised by Algiers. Each parachute drop became the occasion of a sort of village festival. Part of the population went to the designated area and waited for nightfall. Large fires set up to form a T were lit to indicate the direction of ground winds to the pilots. We listened carefully until we could finally hear the rumbling of motors, which grew louder and louder until the airplanes were overhead. The containers were cast off here and there, then collected and transported to barns, where they were opened up: inside were machine guns, strings of bullets, and, on lucky days, parts of heavy machine guns, but also cigarettes, sardines or anchovies, chewing gum, and all sorts of unexpected gadgets. The villagers divvied up the silk, or rather the nylon, from the parachute, which the women used to make delicate blouses. That was the first nylon they had ever touched.

The weak spot in the Vercors fortress was Saint-Nizier, a village on a projecting ledge not far from the rocks of Trois-Pucelles above Grenoble. There the officers tried to create a line of defense as solid as possible. On June 13 a group of Germans filed up, fought for several hours, and then left. The second attack occurred on June 15. There were about two thousand Wehrmacht soldiers and barely three hundred men on our side, who resisted from five to nine o'clock in the morning. But their lines were infiltrated by a war tactic used by the militiamen accompanying the Germans. To understand fully what happened, it is important to remember that a large number of plains residents went up to the Vercors each day to fight alongside the Maquis, who welcomed them warmly. That day, several men had approached the lines claiming they wanted to join the combatants, who let them pass. These men then shot the Vercors defenders from behind, trapping them in the line of fire. This unexpected move completely terrified our men and broke their resistance, already worn very thin, thus exposing the Lans plateau to the troops of the Third Reich. In the words of Paul Dreyfus, they broke down "the carriage entrance."[42] Before leaving the area, the Germans burned much of Saint-Nizier. They had come to test the strength of their adversaries and discovered that our men fought courageously but were not very numerous or well armed. The strategic advantage of the operation was that our lines had been shortened, but the citadel had lost a third of its area and become more vulnerable.

In addition to the military consequences, that operation understandably exacerbated the defenders' anger and their thirst for vengeance. After all, they had been attacked by

Frenchmen paid by the enemy. One of the attackers was shot amid shouting and insults, without any sort of trial, against the wall abutting my parents' house. I didn't have the heart to attend the execution. For a few days afterward, the body of that man, pushed to the side of the road, was frequently kicked by passersby. Such was the exasperation the Vercors people felt at their lack of power.

On June 29 thirty American instructors were dropped by parachute. They were to teach the handling of bazookas, a sort of portable antitank rocket launcher of which the Allies had sent us several samples. The arrival of these instructors was a relief to us, for it meant the superior American command wanted to help the Vercors. My parents, Bernard, and I met a paratrooper from New York and spoke English with him.

During Yves Farge's visit on July 3, a military parade was held in Saint-Martin in his honor. A solemn proclamation on that occasion established the Republic of Vercors. This proclamation states the following: "From this day forth, the decrees of Vichy are abolished and all laws of the Republic renewed. The National Liberation Committee of the Vercors shall enjoy extensive powers. It depends upon the devoted support of the people. Residents of the Vercors, the great Republic has just been reborn on your own home territory. Of this you should be proud. Long live the French Republic! Long live France! Long live General de Gaulle!"

Despite these optimistic words, reality was dismal, and military and civilian leaders of the plateau were deeply worried. There weren't enough seasoned fighters. I remember one of our young friends, whom we called Pierrot and who worked as sentinel. With only a machine gun to protect himself, he was stationed in an appropriate spot in the gorges of the Bourne overlooking a narrow passage. No one could relieve him for nearly forty hours. Having to bear such a responsibility alone without being able to sleep or eat, he was overcome with fatigue. The parachute drops probably made up for all these negative, appalling incidents. On June 23 the pilots dropped multicolored parachutes over Vassieux, as if to attract the Germans' attention. On July 14, 860 containers attached to red, white, and blue parachutes floated down from the sky. All that symbolic sympathy maintained the hope (or rather the illusion) that we would soon receive the arms we needed, and above all the four thousand paratroopers that one of Soustelle's assistants had promised to Chavant in Algiers at the end of May.

While awaiting this arrival, the Vercors staff headquarters received orders to build an airfield near the village of Vassieux to accommodate large airplanes carrying heavy weaponry. The villagers were required to clear away and flatten the ground. People thought the only purpose of such an operation was to create a bridgehead behind enemy troops in the Rhône Valley. But German reconnaissance planes were keeping watch: German bombers attacked Pont-en-Royans on July 8, La Chapelle on July 12. On July 13 the bugles sounded a constant alarm at Vassieux, and planes flew over the village incessantly. Most of the inhabitants fled for cover in the woods.

I am not attempting to write an extensive history of the events of the Vercors, and I am not an expert in military strategy. Rather, I wish to illuminate the events we experienced as individuals by correlating them to the main points of the Vercors resistance. I would not be satisfied writing from the standpoint of Fabrizio del Dongo [in Stendahl's novel *The Charterhouse of Parma*] at Waterloo, for fear of being misunderstood.

Through rumors, we knew that the different elements of the Resistance—the FTP with its communist leanings and the active officers—did not always get along. In Saint-Martin itself, Chavant, the FTP leader, was often at odds with the military, despite his respect for Hervieux and vice versa. In addition, what seemed most tragic was the discrepancy we sensed between the plans of the French military leaders and the Allied command. Had there been true coordination, the Vercors would have received the weapons it needed to accomplish its assigned mission. It was clear that things had fallen apart somewhere and that both the military and the Vercors civilian fighters were going to pay dearly for this dissention or lack of organization.

Some of our officers nevertheless maintained their lightheartedness and taste for gallantry. Despite increasing threats, they decided to celebrate July 14 properly. We were quite surprised to see an officer riding up and down the main street of Saint-Martin early in the morning, dressed in an impeccable uniform with bright yellow gloves, riding a magnificent chestnut horse whose coat had been artfully styled into little diamonds! This vision of elegance and prestige—in the midst of chaos and shortage, and the anguish we all felt, knowing the enemy was about to attack—did little to boost our spirits. Instead, it left us completely demoralized.

Our apprehensions were justified: an hour later, a small, old crate of a plane flew low over the entire plateau, machine-gunning the houses, animals, and people. It made several passes over Saint-Martin, releasing bursts of gunfire that killed peasants in the fields. One of these bursts came through the open window at the post office, and the bullets struck a wall twenty centimeters from Bernard's head. He didn't even have time to be afraid. The villagers spent that July 14 in their cellars. Some way to celebrate the national holiday!

La Chapelle-en-Vercors had been struck hard, with phosphorous bombs. On the evening of July 14 the sky above the mountains was still aglow. It was probably an act of retaliation in response to the major Allied parachute drop that had occurred that very morning at Vassieux: the German planes were keeping a close watch and tried all day to prevent the collection and transport of cylinders. In my diary I noted the courage of the truck drivers overseeing the transport.[43]

Actually, the Germans had prepared their general offensive well before July 14. Vercors leaders were aware of this and kept sending messages of distress, but while it took only seconds for these messages to travel the airways, it took many long hours, even days, for them to travel down the hallway of a building in Algiers. The bureaucracy seriously impeded the functioning of the war machine.

July 21 was D day for the attack. General Pflaum sent his Alpine infantry to attack very narrow passages in the limestone wall running south from Moucherotte. These passages were so difficult to reach (and there were so few men) that one sole company was put in charge of defending the twelve openings. A desperate battle occurred in the south near Die, occupied on July 22. By July 23 the Germans had plunged through the southern gap this created.

Since Villard-de-Lans had been declared an "open city" in an attempt to protect its many children's shelters, the main line of defense to the north passed through Valchevrière. Hervieux sent his best units there, such as the one led by Captain Goderville (Jean Prévost), which included four hundred men and was reinforced by Senegalese soldiers. But it was a desperate fight, given the disproportionate number of combatants (ten to one) and especially the imbalance in weaponry to our disadvantage. For instance, the German troops had a number of mortars, absolutely essential for mountain combat, while the Allies had sent us none at all. The Germans used those mortars to bomb Saint-Martin from Valchevrière on July 23.

Meanwhile, Vassieux was being routed much more severely, owing precisely to the proximity of the airfield we had built there. Early in the morning of July 21, twenty gliders—each bearing the black Iron Cross, escorted by fighters and towed by airplanes—landed on our soil. We were stunned: we had expected Allied planes, and here were Waffen-SS units springing forth from each glider. The inhabitants of the Vercors were devastated. Some tried to escape to the woods; some hit the ground. Enemy gunfire pinned them down. What happened is exactly what Commander Hervieux had sensed when the airfield was being built: "Everything will be fine . . . as long as the Germans don't fling down paratroopers in the middle of the Vercors."

The two companies of Waffen-SS began by destroying the village of Vassieux and set up shop in the ruins of houses, beneath which many residents were caught. The two counterattacks failed completely: with their planes, the Germans had little trouble driving back men who had no artillery or planes to protect themselves. As early as the evening of July 21, a grim discussion on the measures to take was held at headquarters. General Zeller, Chavant, Bousquet, Tanant, and Commander Hervieux were present. Commander Hervieux favored an on-the-spot dispersal: "Go deep into the woods, split up. Since the entire plateau has been infiltrated," he said, "we cannot leave en masse. That would be massacre." On the contrary, Chavant and Bousquet favored a departure en masse in order join the Maquis in Oisans. In the end, Hervieux won—and so much the better, for each time one group of *maquisards* had tried to cross enemy lines to join another, the first group was caught. The dispersion order, agreed upon late in the night of July 21, went into force July 23 at four o'clock in the afternoon.

When all was said and done, Hervieux sent the following message to London: "Vercors defenses pierced the 23rd at 4:00 P.M. after fifty-six hours of battle. Everyone has performed his duty courageously in a desperate struggle, but we are saddened at being obliged to yield because of the enemy's numbers and at having been completely abandoned while the battle was in progress."[44] At about the same time, Chavant, whose style was more direct, sent his own telegraph: "The leaders in Algiers and London do not understand the situation we find ourselves in and can be considered cowards and criminals. We mean what we say: cowards and criminals."[45]

In the afternoon of July 23 the German cannons perched at Valchevrière, facing Saint-Martin, began to bombard Saint-Julien and Saint-Martin. The order to disperse had been given; Bernard had finally been released from his duties. My mother had already waited impatiently for two days, wanting to go to the mountains, but she refused to leave without me and I didn't want to leave Bernard. As for Bernard, he intended to keep working until the end, judging that communications were even more important because the situation was so critical. We therefore left the village at the very last moment with the few other inhabitants who were still there, just as the first shells were falling. We were lucky: no one was hurt, and we arrived in the Briacs in little over half an hour.

There we awaited Monsieur Vignon, a farmer with whom my father had been in touch who was very knowledgeable about the topography of the Vercors, rich in caves and vertical grottos. He led Grandpa and Bernard to one of these roofless caves covered with bushes. That was to be their hiding place: they would sleep at the bottom, on beds of ferns. I had followed Monsieur Vignon to familiarize myself with the path, and it was agreed that I would go every evening, just before nightfall, and bring food to my men. At that hour there was no danger of an ill-timed visit, for the German soldiers were extremely fearful of "terrorists" and did not go out in the mountains at night. If they were to come nosing about in the Briacs during the day, I was to place a tall ladder against a haystack visible from the hiding place in the cave. We believed we were thus prepared for any kind of danger, but we were not: several days later, we learned that the Germans used dogs to track the Maquis. We were terribly frightened, but after consulting the farmers, we sprinkled pepper on the paths leading to the vertical grotto. Pepper apparently throws dogs off the trail. In any case, my father and Bernard were lucky to have someone looking out for them. Many *maquisards* were caught and killed on their way to a source of water.

A little-known incident that may seem silly, had it not occurred under such terrible circumstances, punctuated those first weeks. The German commander, realizing that farmers were taking care of the *maquisards* scattered in the mountains, decided to take away the farmers' cows, leaving only one per family. Toward the end of July, soldiers went to the farms and took the cows away. The soldiers then led them along the road to Villard-de-Lans, where they penned in the enormous herd. The only thing that that fine commander (probably a city dweller!) hadn't considered is that cows need to be milked twice a day. After two days, their udders full to bursting, the cows went crazy with pain and became uncontrollable. The plan that had sprouted in the thick heads of those officers—to lead the cows into Germany—got nowhere near fruition. The cows had to be freed. To the great amazement of their owners, the cows found their own way back to their stables, where they could finally be milked. It seems there is much to be learned in the field of bovine intelligence!

In the Briacs we had no means of communication whatsoever and were unaware of what was happening elsewhere. Several days after our arrival, we were visited by Abbot Gagnol, the parish priest of Vassieux. He was deeply distressed and told us the following story: Being the parish priest, he had dared to enter the village to see what was happening. The Germans said nothing and let him in to have a look. Everything had been destroyed. Nothing moved. All was quiet. There was only a foul odor hanging in the air. But when he passed near a house, he heard someone moaning.

When he went closer, he discovered a little girl, whose leg was caught under a beam, begging him to get her out. She lay on the rotting bodies of her parents. The priest picked her up and carried her to the nearest farm, where they tried to treat her. She said that for six days she had asked the German soldiers who passed nearby to help her, to give her a little water, but not one had answered her pleas. The little girl died of gangrene four days later. I must say that the priest's simple story chilled me to the bone—I was so upset that for a long time I could not think of that incident without crying. Despite the many other horrors the war had shown us, that incident was in a way the epitome of cruelty. It revealed to me clearly the nature of the enemies we were fighting. I will never forget it.

Toward August 8 the Germans left the Vercors. Perhaps they were preparing to confront the Allied troops that were to land in the south of France on August 15, or maybe they badly needed their divisions in Normandy. Once rid of these occupants, the people on the plateau returned to the villages. There they found an unbelievable mess: everything had to be put back in order and repaired, and life had to start over.

Grenoble was liberated on August 22 and Paris on August 25. From then on, we were certain the Allies would be victorious and, with the support of all kinds of resistance groups, would soon be able to end the occupation. As soon as I could, I got the commander's permission to go down to Grenoble in order to obtain the provisions and equipment necessary for survival in the Vercors. After the destruction, burnings, gunfire, and cannon shots, the country was indeed in poor shape. The people suffered not only from the horrors they had witnessed and from their personal losses, but often from the loss of all their property—their houses, furniture, animals, and fodder. I thus became a volunteer social worker. I brought back from Grenoble by truck all sorts of provisions, blankets, and clothing, as well as bricks and cement to start rebuilding. When I arrived I had to divide up these treasures among the needy. This sometimes caused quite a few problems. While I was doing that exhausting work, I heard that certain villagers accused me of taking advantage of my position to serve myself first. I thus learned firsthand that a selfless act is rarely understood as such: people project onto others the attitude they would have in a similar situation.

That is how our stay in the Vercors ended. While it is true that neither Bernard nor I tried actively to get caught up in that battle, the minute that circumstances drew us in, we did the right thing. Bernard in particular had never before dreamed of joining a band of *maquisards*. He was pessimistic about his own capabilities and thought he would not be able to live a life so foreign to his ways. But as soon as volunteers were requested in Saint-Martin, he stepped forward and did his job with his usual meticulousness. He never flinched, even in the worst danger. I am not claiming he was a hero; I am merely touched by his simple courage.

As for me, I remember constantly being involved in what was happening. I had a part in the action and even felt a sort of excitement mixed with anxiety. The depression in which I had floundered since 1940 therefore dissipated in the heat of collective action. It is likely that had I joined the Resistance earlier, the necessity of daily action would perhaps have cured my melancholy. Since I did not believe I could, I will never have the satisfaction of knowing for sure.

THREE

The Postwar Years

We left Saint-Martin to go back to Paris at the beginning of October. Finally, we would be able to return to our apartment on Rue Vésale, to our books, our friends, our life. Readapting was, nonetheless, difficult: after leaving the Dauphiné, where we had been immersed in the violence of combat and the atrocities of war, we were suddenly faced with the problems of civilian life and were unable to get our bearings. It was still very difficult to find food and keep warm. The Germans had systematically drained France of its raw materials and food products. But what was most difficult for us was getting back to our studies. Of course, Bernard had never completely interrupted his work, but he still had the biggest part left, the part he dreaded most—the *agrégation* [highest exams for teachers]. As for me, I had not done any philosophy for three years. I had been completely cut off from any sort of intellectual work. Since I was also suffering from emotional shock, I could not manage to regain an interest in my studies. But I had to get back to them, in order to obtain a certificate in the sciences and my diploma (the equivalent of today's master's degree). I selected as my topic "The Relationship between the Finite and the Infinite in Spinozist Philosophy" and chose Henri Gouhier as my advisor.

The war was not yet over. It continued in the East, and the Americans were battling the formidable Japanese in the Pacific. The counterattack in the Ardennes rattled Europe in February 1945. We wondered whether the forceful reaction of those we thought were already defeated might foreshadow a serious reversal. Luckily, our worries were unfounded: in several weeks the Allies continued their march toward Berlin, where they were to meet the Soviet troops.

The stories and photographs of the concentration camps affected us deeply. Of course, we had sensed deep down that we would never again see our deported family members, having had no news of them since their departure. But we could not imagine the atrocious nightmare of their life in the extermination camps, for that was utterly unimaginable. When they entered those camps, Allied soldiers discovered conditions beyond what a human being can stand.

When you come back from war
or somewhere else,
somewhere else
where you spoke with Death,
it's hard to come back
and learn to speak with the living.
When you've looked Death
square in the eye,
it's hard to relearn

to look at the living
with their impenetrable eyes.¹

Shortly thereafter, the photos taken by the Allies were exhibited in public. We knew then that neither my grandfather nor Cécile was ever coming back. We had to live the rest of our lives burdened by the knowledge that what we knew was nothing compared to the horrors that our friends, relatives, and so many strangers had experienced. "The concentrationary universe shrivels away within itself," writes David Rousset. "It still lives on in the world like a dead planet laden with corpses. Normal men do not know that everything is possible. Even if the evidence forces their intelligence to admit it, their muscles do not believe it. . . . Death lived among the concentrationees at every hour of their existence."²

Georges was alive. His parents were dead. When he was very little, he was told his father had "died in the war," but my parents were unable to tell him anything about his mother, Cécile, for they knew nothing of her fate. When Georges returned to Paris in March 1945, he was nine years old. He asked no questions, but his silence had to be answered; he had to be told why his mother was not there. My mother probably had a talk with him. Or maybe not. There is no way of knowing, since neither Georges nor my mother ever spoke of it, and now both of them are dead. Not knowing seemed so inconceivable that I recently asked several of Georges's close friends. None of them could tell me. It's as if a black hole had opened up at the core of my cousin's being, a crater that only the most absolute silence could protect. Nowhere, in none of his books, does Georges tell how his mother's death at Auschwitz was revealed to him. In *W, or the Memory of Childhood* he nevertheless expresses it indirectly, sidestepping the issue: "Later on, my aunt took me to see an exhibition about concentration camps. It was being held somewhere near La Motte-Piquet-Grenelle. . . . I remember the photographs of the walls of the gas chambers showing scratchmarks made by the victims' fingernails, and a set of chessmen made from bits of bread."[3]

My nervous state continued to complicate my life and upset me. Sometimes the anguish gripped me so tightly it seemed I was pinned to a corner of my bed, unable to get up, refusing to wash and do my hair, with no appetite. During these difficult states, which lasted several weeks, I could not read anything, for no word, no text made any sense. I could not see anyone or do anything. The most minor decision was a problem. At the same time I felt as though my feelings were drying up, which troubled me. After a certain amount of time—I could never predict how long—I would start to feel better. Slowly, I would become more cheerful, regain the desire to be active and the ability to work. I was once again positive, optimistic. It seemed as if everything was easy, as it had been before. I would rush to my desk to make up for lost time. Then the cycle would begin all over again.

Such mood swings are described in psychiatry manuals: when serious, they are called manic-depressive psychosis, but they exist in varying degrees. When I studied psychopathology at Sainte-Anne Hospital, I observed real melancholiacs and women in acute manic states. I worried I was sliding downhill and would end up in the hospital. I attributed my emotional imbalance to a sort of explosion of all the angst that had built up inside me during the war; I also thought my break with Sartre and Simone de Beauvoir had significantly contributed to it.

Bernard was of course very worried, and so were my parents. But when my angst was in remission, I finished writing my thesis and somehow managed to obtain my certificate of ethnology. At the beginning of the 1945 academic year, my condition was still the same. This made it difficult to plan for my *agrégation*. I therefore consulted a psychoanalyst, Doctor Pasche. At about the same time, I felt like seeing Simone de Beauvoir again. Perhaps my desire to see her was related to my starting therapy. We probably met during one of my frequent black periods, because she was quite startled. When Sartre was en route for his second trip to the United States, she wrote him: "I'm upset about Bianca Bienenfeld. . . . She moved me—and filled me with remorse—because she's suffering from an intense and dreadful attack of neurasthenia, and it's our fault, I think. It's the very indirect, but profound, after-shock of the business between her and us. She's the only person to whom we've really done harm, but we have harmed her. . . . She weeps all the time—she wept three times during the dinner, and she weeps at home when she has to read a book or go to the kitchen to eat. . . . She's terribly unhappy, and extremely lucid without her lucidity getting her anywhere. At times, she really looked quite mad."[4]

My deep distress must really have touched her and made a lasting impression, for she invited me to begin a new friendship, which I could count on but which would, of course, have none of the passion of our former relationship.

I accepted wholeheartedly. From that day on, and for forty years, we saw each other about once a month in various restaurants she took me to. From time to time, but not very often, she came to eat at my place. Generally, it was as follows: She would call me to make a date and reserve a table at the restaurant of her choice. I would pick her up by car, especially in the last years of her life when she could barely walk. That way, I could take her home. I set the rule that she be the one to call and not I, for I didn't want it to appear as if I were always the one asking (or begging). I wanted to see her only when she wished and only when she was available. In any case, she was much busier than I, and it was only natural that she remain the one in charge.

These details show just how many inaccuracies Deirdre Bair's biography of Simone de Beauvoir contains. In fact, Simone de Beauvoir herself was probably the source of some of these errors. She must have lied to her biographer that she had "not been in touch with Bianca for years."[5] Simone de Beauvoir had every reason to minimize my role in her life and Sartre's. At first she promised me never to mention my name in writing or speaking. Above all, she felt enough remorse toward me to try instinctively to erase what had united us and what had split us apart. Since Deirdre Bair never checked with me, Simone de Beauvoir could tell her whatever she wanted, including that I wanted to divorce Bernard, then a little later that I *had* divorced him.[6] This is pure invention: divorce was never an issue for Bernard and me. On the contrary, our relationship continued to grow closer and richer. Such assertions deeply shocked me. A serious biographer should not have taken her subject of study at her word. She should have backed her subject's words with other accounts, as much as possible. After all, I reside in Paris, where I worked until 1983. I still live here. It would have been easy to find me.

But to get back to the true relationship that existed between Simone de Beauvoir and me during all those years: One may be surprised—and rightly so—that I began a new relationship with her. After all, she had been very harsh toward me. She had broken our friendship at a time when I really needed her. Then, during all those years of war when the Jews were being hunted down, she never tried to find out whether I was alive, deported, or dead. I could thus have had many grievances against her. But it was against Sartre that I bore the deeper grudge, because of how he had treated me and because of his indifference, which seemed so deep it was painful. Although breaking with the Beaver had been more sudden, it happened with relative clarity: I had, of course, understood that her relationship with Bost was a lot older than she had confessed, and that had hurt me. But I was well aware that any surge of emotion is based on a free choice; it is spontaneous, irrepressible, and fundamentally fragile, even if it lasts. That is what I thought *after* my double passion had collapsed and its illusions had dissipated: I had finally learned a lesson in reality. As Freud would have said, I had passed from the pleasure principle to the reality principle. If only I had had that realization at the time I believed the threesome was unshakable.

My love for the Beaver during my early adulthood had been so deep that I naturally turned toward her during that difficult postwar period of my life. At the same time, however,

I sensed she was a potential danger. I felt this during my first pregnancy, in 1946. I was afraid that the child I was carrying might one day suffer the effects of my troubled youth. I was all the more worried, seeing that Simone de Beauvoir had written a novel, *She Came to Stay*, and Sartre *The Age of Reason*, followed by *The Reprieve*, in which the main character is based on Olga Kosakievicz.[7] I did not know what Olga thought, but I was horrified at the idea that the same thing could happen to me. After being held up to ridicule in real life, there was no way I was going to become "material for a novel." I therefore asked them to come see me. We met in the Jardins du Ranelagh in the summer. I explained to them that I wanted their solemn oath never to quote me in any of their books or to model a character after me. Annoyed and bored, they gave in and promised. What made that entire conversation seem comical was their reaction to my big belly: it was as if I were a slug or some other disgusting animal. They gazed nervously straight ahead. I always knew they had this attitude. They found motherhood, which brings into play organic forces and fluids, deeply revolting.

It is therefore rather difficult to understand the complex nature of our relationship. I had to get to know another Beaver, probably matured by the war but still the same in many ways. I myself had changed because I had experienced some very difficult situations, because even after that time of death I had decided to have a baby. We had to try to establish a satisfactory relationship between us. Whether we ended up clashing or becoming closer, we were going to test our mutual desire to mend broken ties.

But it was clear to me that our new friendship was poisoned from the outset by memories of the past. It was impossible for us to discuss it. Impossible for me, because I had been too passionate about an unhappy love affair whose development I did not wish to analyze with her. Impossible for her, perhaps because she imagined that the least bit of encouragement would rekindle my feelings, although this was completely out of the question because my life was permanently focused elsewhere. The brutal blow I had received in 1940 had at least taught me not to live with my head in the clouds. It was a rude awakening, and for me the passion was over (although maybe not the naïveté). I had also learned to settle for what I was given.

Nevertheless, the Beaver's reserve was based primarily on the very substance of our past. No wonder I failed to understand this: I had no idea whatsoever of her true feelings toward me, of her scheming, or her lies. Everything I discovered in 1990 was impossible for me to have known in 1945 or 1960. She was obliged to continue lying, like a prisoner of her past hypocrisy. But I never sensed her duplicity. All that I knew was that we could not speak of the past, so heavy, so present between us. The stench of the dead "threesome" hung in the air but never permeated our conversations. "How to get rid of it . . ." Ionesco would have wondered.[8] She probably feared I would blame her and she would not be able to hide completely what I still wasn't supposed to know. It was therefore better to keep quiet. If by accident I mentioned a place we had once gone, she would blush slightly and change the subject.

The strictly regulated nature of our relationship gave me the impression she felt obligated, and I was sad to think she saw me only in remembrance of our former friendship or in order to make up for hurting me in the past.

In addition to this implicit refusal to discuss what had happened in 1940, we often let misunderstandings slide. Aware that our confrontations might have become violent, we deliberately avoided conflict with each other.

One of the issues that divided us was her scorn toward the bourgeoisie. Of course, her background was as bourgeois as my own—even more so, if such things can be measured. But she believed that her revolt against her family's origins, customs, and beliefs was enough to whitewash her. She joined with Sartre, who confused his hatred for his stepfather with hatred of the entire bourgeoisie. As an intellectual, she believed she was no longer part of the middle class, with its solid traditions, simply because she rejected it.

I never felt as clearly as she did the distance that separated me from the principles of the middle class. If one of the constants of the bourgeoisie is its relationship to money, my family was completely different from some French bourgeois families, for whom money was the core of their existence in society. When fate brought them security and affluence, my parents, victims of the tribulations of Jewish life, accepted it simply and appreciatively. But they were ready to become poor again, for they were not bound to money. I had no qualms about being bourgeois, which did not prevent me from being lucid. While I gave no value to appearances or to how wealthy people were, I saw no reason to fake being a blue-collar worker (as did Simone Weil) or a farmer, as did all those young people who went to the country in 1968 to raise goats. I felt no guilt whatsoever and saved my strength for what I considered worthier battles.

Another thing that came between us was her loyalty to

Sartre's positions. He could not help spicing up his public actions with a dose of drama I found excessive; he exaggerated. Consider the Bertrand Russell War Crimes Tribunal, which Sartre cofounded with the British philosopher Lord Bertrand Russell. This court judged infamous dictators using ample testimony but was unable to apply any verdict whatsoever. Consider also the scandal Sartre caused when he refused the Nobel Prize, claiming he did not want to buy a suit or shake hands with the king of Sweden. Although Simone de Beauvoir did not have the same troubled nature, she followed Sartre docilely, rather sadly, sometimes surprised, always prepared to join in; Sartre was the master who decided everything.

There were many other topics on which we sharply disagreed. Of all that the Beaver had tried to teach me, one lesson in particular had not been assimilated. I was married. She must have thought that in so doing I had proved myself to be a bourgeois woman. (As if only bourgeois women married and had children!) From the Beaver's point of view, marrying Bernard was a sort of regression. For proof, one need only page through *Letters to Sartre* and feel her simmering frustration, rage, and vengefulness. She tried to make a fool of me and, what I consider more serious, to make a fool of Bernard with the ugliest malice. This shows that her contempt of marriage was not simply the refusal of a traditional institution but a rejection based on personal feelings.

Indeed, we never spoke of Bernard, of my love and admiration for him. It was almost as if he had never existed. She probably wondered why I continued to live with him, to make him happy, for she professed that boredom is the rule for all marriages: "There are many marriages that 'go well'—that is to say, in which man and wife reach a compromise.... But there is one curse they very rarely escape: it is boredom."[9] Between Bernard and me there was no boredom, no cheating, no mistrust. There was only physical attraction, deep love, friendship, trust. The Beaver's prejudices toward marriage made her unable to accept these facts. This explains why she invented the story of my divorce for Bair and also why she was so surprised by the signs of my distress during Bernard's sickness and death.

The issue of children separated us perhaps even more: having never felt the desire to have a child, Simone de Beauvoir could not imagine what drives a man and a woman to want children. For example, with regard to pregnancy, she writes in *The Second Sex* that a woman "and the child with which she is swollen make up together an equivocal pair overwhelmed by life. Ensnared by nature, the pregnant woman is plant and animal.... She is a human being, a conscious and free individual, who has become life's passive instrument." Even more vividly, she describes the pregnant woman as a being in which "day after day a growth arising from her flesh but foreign to it is going to enlarge within her; she is the prey of the species."[10] These few quotes demonstrate clearly that this purely physical perspective of motherhood is but a kind of spiritualism in reverse. According to her, a human being demeans itself morally and spiritually by letting itself succumb to reproductive instincts. There is almost a metaphysical conflict between Nature and the Mind. All the deep, positive significance of wanting a child is, if not left completely unaddressed, expressed only weakly, as though begrudgingly, whereas the disgust, fear, and hatred of motherhood—as perceived by Simone de Beauvoir—are expressed forcefully. If one knew only these texts from *The Second Sex*, it would come as a surprise to discover that existentialism is a deeply spiritual philosophy.

As for me, raising my two daughters was a constant joy, even when it caused me fatigue and worry. Perhaps I was wrong in telling the Beaver about my worries in particular and not enough about the deep, warm feelings I had for them. Sometimes I would bring her photos. She flipped through them rapidly, nervously, murmuring with irritation, "They're very cute, very cute." When my daughters were older, they began to hold her attention more. I would sometime tell her of my difficulties in my relationships with them, which we would discuss. She always tried to alleviate my worries, but I could feel that she was torn between her friendship for me and her automatic sympathy for adolescents grappling with the difficulties of tearing themselves away from the family unit.

One day I had had enough of the lack of any kind of connection between the writers I knew and my family. I suggested the Beaver ask Sartre if he would like to meet my daughters and see Bernard again. If so, she should invite us all to lunch. They accepted. I probably had a vague desire to show them the beauty and intelligence of the individuals I had brought into the world—there was a certain defiance in my actions.

Sartre and the Beaver waited for us—Bernard, Marianne, Sylvia, and me—in a restaurant on Boulevard Montparnasse. Marianne was eighteen years old, Sylvia was thirteen. Lunch went fairly well. Sartre, very animated and in brilliant form, often addressed Marianne, who was stunning, or Bernard and me, whom he had not seen for a long time. That was a short time after *The Words* was published, in 1964. I remember, because that book received unanimous praise in the press as a marvelously well written, true masterpiece. Sartre asked me what I thought of it. Well, I didn't think too much of it, aside from his brilliant style. I answered rather vehemently that I thought the tone of the autobiography rang false and that, in particular, he had depicted his mother in an unnecessarily cruel manner, reducing her to nothing but a little girl with no personality who deferred to his father. I added that, as for how he portrayed himself, he seemed to enjoy denigrating himself, distancing himself from the child he once had been, as though he wanted to dissociate himself, to beat himself up with his own stick. It all seemed like a show, nothing but an act. Interested and amused, Sartre listened to me (he loved to be critiqued) but affirmed his love for his mother. He asked me to give him credit at least for his sincerity in writing the book. Knowing what he thought of sincerity in general and of literary sincerity in particular, his defense seems awfully weak to me.

Continually avoiding arguments, as the Beaver and I got into the habit of doing, can have unexpected and negative long-term effects. That was the case in autumn 1982 (two years after Sartre's death). A bitter conflict revealed how many reservations the Beaver had about me—vicious reservations that I had never suspected. Because that summer I traveled to Mexico, I was far away when the terrorist attack on Goldenberg's restaurant on Rue des Rosiers occurred. While in Mexico City I tried to make sense of the story in the local press regarding the event but, not knowing Spanish, I probably did not understand it completely. When I saw the Beaver again at the start of the school year, the topic came up in our conversation. I said something about "the bomb that destroyed Goldenberg's restaurant." Immediately, as if she had been cut to the quick, she flew into a rage and said, "So you don't know it was a machine gun attack, not a bombing. In any case, you don't give a damn what happens to other Jews. You don't even have a basic sense of solidarity with your people!" I was dumbfounded. I tried to explain that I had been in Mexico City when the attack occurred; that was the reason for my error. Besides, I did not see what gave her the right to state that I felt no solidarity with other Jews. Misstating a detail of the incident was not important: what difference is there, anyway, between a bomb and a machine gun? Both wound and kill. She barely listened to me. I could tell she was irritated with me, without knowing why.

Once I got home, I wrote her a letter to explain things again. I also addressed the question of Palestine, because it seemed to me, on reflection, that our misunderstanding about Rue des Rosiers actually stemmed from our differences regarding the Palestinian problem. Strangely enough, the Beaver was unconditionally pro-Israel, while I was much more critical of Israel's politics. It seemed to me that they led to an impasse, a serious matter for both the Palestinians and for Israel, whose existence in the midst of so many Arab peoples was still in jeopardy. I had formed my beliefs a long time ago, and they surely hinged upon my experience during the Algerian War, which made me aware of the difficult relations that can exist between a less developed people and a technically advanced people. I was trying to reconcile my various political stances. Contrary to what the Beaver thought, I was not pro-Palestine—I simply *also* considered the point of view of the Palestinians, against whom a basic injustice had been originally committed, an injustice the Israelis should have taken into account.

Here is her reply:

Dear Bianca,

I'm answering your letter so that you don't think I read it indifferently, but it's stupid. Since the situation is "ambiguous," as you say, why would I bear any sort of grudge or scorn toward someone who doesn't share my opinions?

As for Lanzmann,[11] *I don't want to talk about him. But I did notice that all you can do is insult him by saying he can do nothing but insult others. I'm sorry you subscribe to the chauvinist prejudice that a woman is able to form her ideas only from a man's. I have many friends (female friends) who don't know Lanzmann and still share my point of view. But not to worry, you're not alone. You should know that the majority of the Left intelligentsia is radically pro-Palestine and is more than happy to use Lebanon to condemn Israel one more time.*

What shocked me most in our conversation is the lack of information that made you speak of a "bomb" on Rue des Rosiers. And also your indifference. Does your severity toward Israel cause you to reject any sort of solidarity with Jews as a whole?

This said, you shouldn't turn all our arguments into

tragedies. If you did, we would no longer be able to speak to each other.

See you soon. Kisses.[12]

I do not wish to comment on this letter; I leave it for the reader to judge. I will say only that it was Simone de Beauvoir, through her totally unjustified attacks, who made that minor incident into a tragedy; she insulted me and not vice versa. Furthermore, the Jewish question must have been a very delicate issue for her. Indeed, when one confronts this strange sensitivity, this unexpected quirk in her attitude during the war as revealed in *Letters to Sartre*, one is struck by the guilt beneath her apparent intransigence.

Our relationship was thus very complicated. She was surely concerned about my loyalty to her, for many people detested her. This amazed and saddened her: "They all hate us." She who dreamed of being loved could not understand how her own verbal violence, like Sartre's, could cause her adversaries to hate her.

It is therefore certain that something besides guilt attached her to me. If not, she would not have continued to see me for forty years. She was too harsh and too selfish with her time for that. Suffice it to say that her feelings toward me were ambiguous, as they had been in the past.

We did agree completely on several important issues. We firmly rejected colonialist domination, a political concept still ingrained in the French mentality, even on the Left. *Les temps modernes* was virtually alone in opposing the war in Indochina in the 1950s. When the revolt occurred in

Algeria, the commitment of Sartre and his friends did not waver. As for Bernard and me, we were soon very concerned by the turn of events. Our first teaching positions had been in Algiers between 1948 and September 1954.[13] We were aware that there were various nationalist movements, that there had been violently quashed revolts, as in Sétif. But when the tremors of what was to become the "dirty war" in Algeria began to be felt, we had already been transferred to Paris.

Living on the other side of the Mediterranean had made me particularly sensitive to what was happening there. I participated in the conflict out of sympathy, because I was anticolonialist and believed that after Morocco and Tunisia had won their independence, it would be futile to claim that "Algeria is/was France." It seemed to me that the general course of history in the mid-twentieth century made the eventual independence of the Algerian people inevitable. But I was also aware that the Algerian Europeans who desperately refused Algerian independence (those who were later called *pieds-noirs*) did so out of love of a land they had cultivated themselves. What struck me was their ignorance of history, their refusal to consider the world around them. I foresaw that their blindness would lead them into tragedy. Furthermore, I had always opposed the scornful attitude most Europeans bore toward Arab populations. For all these reasons, I was as sympathetic toward the people in revolt as I was toward Algerian-born French people.

The first massacres and the first bombings of what was still called only a rebellion occurred on All Saints' Day in 1954. With anguish we followed the series of attacks and the ensuing repression in 1955 and 1956. In autumn 1956 a plane traveling from Morocco to Tunisia carrying several Algerian leaders, including Ben Bella, was intercepted in Algerian air space, despite the French government's assurance to the Moroccan sultan that his guests were safe. That incident made waves all over the world. We spoke of it a lot at school. During a union meeting, one of my colleagues complained about the general indifference toward the military's actions: her husband, a doctor, had just been called up to serve in Algeria. Her indignation touched me and sparked my decision to act. That was the beginning of my involvement in the opposition to that war. With the help of some colleagues, I drafted the following petition:

"The undersigned employees of Lycée La Fontaine request that the government take the steps necessary to negotiate an effective cease-fire in Algeria as soon as possible. Only through negotiation will it be possible to lay the groundwork for a peaceful policy and establish new, mutually consented relations between France and Algeria."

This appeal was immediately signed by over half the teachers and administrators of the lycée. It was then passed from school to school in Paris and the surrounding areas. In several weeks, I had over one thousand signatures. I found that result encouraging and believed it meant that a large portion of the teaching body was against continuing the colonial war. What was true of secondary school teachers had to be true of other sections of the population. I therefore sent the petition to the government, also addressing it to General de Gaulle, who had retired to Colombey-les-Deux-Eglises. I received no reply from Guy Mollet[14] (should this have surprised me?), but General de Gaulle did send a little card saying that my letter had interested him.

I do not intend to give a detailed account of all the steps we took, all our actions, all the colloquia we organized during the five and a half years of that war, up to the Evian Accords. I wish only to indicate that in the beginning, at a meeting of the Comités des Lycées held at Le Cluny café, we organized a single committee to include everyone in secondary education who supported negotiations with Algeria. It was called the University Vigilance Committee for the Defense of Freedom and Peace in Algeria,[15] and the secretariat was made up of Madeleine Rebérioux, Andrée Tournès, Geneviève Trimouille, and myself. The committee remained in close contact with the Comité Audin, created after the death of Maurice Audin, with the Colloque Universitaire, and many other organizations. Added to our teaching and family life was the demanding work of coordinating and organizing action. We were appalled that all the political parties accepted the continuation of a war they did not even want to call a war. Most French people could not have cared less; their indifference fueled our anger.

Simone de Beauvoir and her friends were on the same side as we were. However, she was perhaps more disgusted with France and the French than we were,[16] because at first she had not perceived the size of the protest movement. But little by little she became caught up in various initiatives and signed protests, the most important of which was the "Appel des 121."[17] Finally, having been notified by Gisèle Halimi, she participated in the Comité Djamila Boupacha, named after a young Algerian girl who had been frightfully tortured. It can thus be said that Simone de Beauvoir and I had finally found common political ground. This tie between us strengthened our friendship.

Bernard's death in September 1978 gave me another chance to measure our friendship. I buried my distress deep inside: I refused to let myself cry even though I was ravaged by sorrow because a whole piece of my life had just been torn away. We had lived together for thirty-seven years. During that time we had never left each other's side. Our love had grown and deepened over the years.

Despite my sorrow, or because of it, I dove into the mass of papers he had written. He had specialized in the aesthetics of art, which he taught at the University of Paris-I, and had begun extensive research for his thesis. He had worked on it for nearly sixteen years. Death had seized him suddenly before he could finish it. It seemed unacceptable to let the result of such perseverance, of so much science and sensitivity, stagnate at the bottom of a drawer without trying to get it published. His long study covered the complex relationship between time and painting. I was of course familiar with the main ideas, which we had often discussed, but Bernard did not like to show me what he had written before finishing it. I therefore knew only what he had typed—about half of it (600 pages). The rest was nearly illegible scribbling with no notes about the organization. I decided to begin by typing up everything, a task that took me almost two years (I was still teaching at the lycée at the time). I ended up with a mass of 1,250 pages, an achievement that did not fail to frighten me.

My training is in philosophy, and I like the arts, especially painting, but I am not a specialist in aesthetics. I thus faced a big problem: I had to judge a heavy manuscript on the philosophy of art, even though it was not my thing. I asked Bernard's colleagues and friends for help but found none. All of them had so many different activities, books to write, and colloquia to attend that they made excuses and declined. One of them went so far as to try to destroy, with unjustified criticism, any confidence I might have had in my husband's work. I seethed with rage. Had I been weaker or shyer, I could very well have given it all up that day and sunk into a depression. Luckily, I explode when treated unfairly. Spurred on by this incident, I fought even harder to achieve my goal: to get Bernard's work published.

Of all our friends, only Marie-Louise and Henri Gouhier (the latter had been our history of philosophy professor at the Sorbonne) were willing to read the fat manuscript and give me their opinion, which was complimentary. But I needed more than one opinion before delving into a task I expected to be long and full of pitfalls. I asked the Beaver whether she would be willing to read the text and tell me what she thought of it. She was, of course, not a specialist in aesthetics, but she liked painting, and I judged her to be exactly the kind of reader who might be interested in Bernard's ideas.

She ordinarily read a lot very quickly. She was not afraid of 1,250 pages and read them twice. Her impression was very positive. She found the analyses of paintings very interesting. Moreover, she thought the main thesis was completely new and solid: to look at painting from a temporal point of view, both in the way works were perceived and what they actually contained. This appraisal was extremely important to me—it gave me the courage to begin work on the difficult task that awaited me. But Simone de Beauvoir went even further: she volunteered to show the manuscript to Robert Gallimard,[18] with whom she was friendly. He went to her place himself to pick up the heavy mass of papers. In discussing the work with him, she expressed the interest and novelty of the ideas it developed.

Mr. Gallimard called me into his office several weeks later to tell me politely but firmly that the text was unpublishable. I was not surprised in the least, but I was shocked that he gave me no advice on how to make it publishable, no advice on what to aim for or the steps to take to achieve this aim. Such a reaction was disappointing, but his bluntness made me understand that I could never hope to publish the work as it was—remarkable but too long. I therefore went back to work on it for two more years, having decided to cut out the expositions that Bernard tended to overillustrate. I also eliminated several analyses of paintings. I had to cut out sentences, paragraphs, and even entire pages while still maintaining the style and especially the ideas developed by the author.

That prolonged contact with Bernard's writing and thought did help me recover from his death. I was not faced with pure and simple emptiness but continued instead to work together with the one I had loved. Most of all, I felt as though I was doing something for him. That work on a text that was both close to my heart but not my own, however, was very painful and cost me emotionally and intellectually. I constantly had to make delicate choices with no one to guide me. I lived in doubt but forged ahead boldly. I had no choice: it was all or nothing.

Thus cleaned up, lightened, and illustrated with reproductions I had carefully chosen, *Peinture et temps*[19] was published in 1983 by Klincksieck and reprinted in 1987 with additional chapters on cubism and futurism that could not be included in the first edition.

I have retold this episode at some length, first of all because developing Bernard's book was very important for me, in many respects. I had accomplished a task full of risks: not only had the book been published, but it was selling. My daughters and friends were proud of me. The enormous amount of work the author had done was now accessible to the public. But I have told this story for another reason as well: That was a time when I truly felt the Beaver's affection. She had begun to understand the workings of my life; she had sensed that Bernard had truly been someone I loved, and she was moved by my fight to save his book.

To get back to Simone de Beauvoir, I would like to describe a day involving "the taxi," an essential tool in her life. She always traveled by taxi, since for a long time she could no longer walk—or no longer wanted to walk. In addition, she never took public transportation. For one of our visits, we were to meet at Chez Pierre, a nice restaurant on Rue de Richelieu near the Théâtre Français. Since taxis were on strike that day, I simply took the Metro. I waited a long time for her. When she finally arrived, out of breath and dishevelled, she told me she had had a heck of a time finding a car and the driver had left her far away, near the Tuileries, fearing the reprisal of his colleagues crowded around the Palais Royal. I was saddened to see her in such a state after walking about three blocks. We both silently dreaded the return trip. I offered to get my car and drive her home, but she refused. Besides, the traffic jam at the Palais Royal was such that even buses could not move. The only solution left was the Metro. It had surely been over twenty years since she had ridden in it. The first problem was that the Beaver hated going down stairs: it made her slightly dizzy, and she would place her foot on each step with extreme caution. It had always been like that. We carefully descended the stairs at Palais Royal station. When we had to transfer at Place d'Italie, I supported her heavy body the best I could. The walk through the endless passageways was perilous enough, but the worst was when we arrived at Denfert-Rochereau, a station very deep underground: she flatly refused to take the escalator, so I had to heave her up, step by step, to the exit. Once we got to her place, where she had a meeting with a journalist, she collapsed onto her couch, out of breath and completely exhausted. I took leave of her as though we had been through a major ordeal, which had left me with the painful realization of my friend's declining physical condition.

That incident leads me to discuss our opposing attitudes about health. I had always been very concerned about my own health and the health of others, while she had always been indifferent and even hostile to my advice to take care of herself. Of course, when she was young, she had been strong and resilient, subjecting her body to difficult trials. I admired her courage, arising both from the need to expend energy and a true love of nature. Because of her vibrant vitality, she was never aware of the limits of her strength. She would sometimes leave for a long hike with only a chocolate bar in her pocket. She wanted to travel all over the world. With its inevitable constraints, her body was both a vehicle to achieve her desires and an obstacle to be conquered by sheer willpower.

My own health, on the contrary, had been very fragile when I was a small child. With the attentive care of my parents, I surmounted my weakness. My father, who had not forgotten his medical studies, instilled in me a special concern for my lifestyle: I became strong and athletic. Perhaps these circumstances explain my continued interest in physical well-being and medical problems in general.

When the Beaver grew older and focused all her energy on intellectual pursuits, she stopped all physical exercise. She no longer wanted to go on bike rides, which she had so loved, or on walks. The only law she lived by was to do whatever she pleased, which was to be physically lazy. When I tried to talk to her about it, she would reply childishly that she did not feel like it anymore. When I tried to tell her that the abuse of alcohol would ravage her body, she would become irritated and pay no attention to my advice. It was as if my prudence and concern for her were a sort of crime.

She had very particular eating habits. At restaurants she insisted she be served no cream, no butter, no giblets or organ meats; she refused to eat cheese. In a word, she was disgusted by anything made from milk. I thought this refusal was full of meaning and was related to her rejection of motherhood. Perhaps something significant had happened to her as a small child. In pondering these questions, I reread the beginning of *Memoirs of a Dutiful Daughter*. I noticed that between the first sentence, "I was born at four o'clock in the morning on the 9th of January 1908,"[20] and the second, describing a photo in which a group of ladies and gentlemen are smiling at a beautiful baby—that is to say, between the registry office and a narcissistic image—there is *nothing* describing the very important sensual relationship between a newborn and its mother. In general, family stories compensate for the lack of early memories. Later, she describes the terrifying ritual of mealtime: "The principal function of Louise and Mama was to feed me: their task was not always an easy one. The world became more intimately part of me when it entered through my mouth than through my eyes and my sense of touch. I would not accept it entirely. The insipidity of milk puddings, porridge, and mashes of bread and butter made me burst into tears; the oiliness of fat meat and the clammy mysteries of shellfish revolted me; tears, screams, vomitings: my repugnance was so deeply rooted that in the end they gave up trying to force me to eat those disgusting things."[21]

During her last years, when ordering food she would carefully choose the wine we would drink, and I always reminded her (to no avail) that while I liked wine a lot, I drank very little: a half bottle would be enough. But she would impatiently brush aside my comment and order a full bottle, drinking nearly all of it herself and eating very little. As the years passed, and especially during Sartre's illness, I realized to my dismay that Simone de Beauvoir was becoming truly anorectic. After mulling over what to choose, she would slowly eat a few forkfuls before pushing away her plate. But I could never stop her from finishing a bottle. If, while she was making out the check, I motioned for the waiter to take away the bottle when there was still a glassful left, she would stop me angrily and drink all the wine to the last drop. Since I knew her doctor had enjoined her to strictly limit her daily alcohol intake, and since she had probably gulped down one or two whiskeys before the meal, I was very worried to see her subsisting on alcohol alone. She had tried in vain to fight Sartre's alcoholism; now Sylvie le Bon was trying to fight the Beaver's and was faring no better. I sometimes called Sylvie to tell her about a particularly alarming incident. She generally replied sourly that she was doing her best to watch over the Beaver, but that she could not be at her side constantly. She completely misjudged my intentions: I did not blame her in the least and was not minimizing the difficulty of her task. I just thought it might be helpful for her to know.

There is no doubt that Simone de Beauvoir's tendency to take refuge in alcohol resulted from the difficult ordeal she faced. She was deeply distraught and saddened by Sartre's health. Her affection and pity for him and her own panic about losing him were tearing her apart.

But something else was upsetting her, too. It was the way death was working its way into him. Simone de Beauvoir had always been terrified of death and haunted by obsessive fear of her own end. She could not accept without violent metaphysical protest that a consciousness, her own consciousness in particular, could disappear suddenly, taking with it a world of experience, thought, and pleasure. But life's ordeals had modified this extreme point of view. This was first apparent during her mother's illness and her "very easy" death, a deeply emotional experience for her. Sitting at her tortured mother's bedside, the Beaver rediscovered her affection for her mother, now mixed with pity. The nearness of the end caused her to think about death and almost accustomed her to its presence, despite her fears and the difficulties she had to confront with the doctors and nurses.[22]

Her attitude toward death nevertheless changed even more significantly during Sartre's illness, which dislodged her long-standing egocentrism and pushed her toward concern for another person. Her love for Sartre thus helped her to destroy the boundary of her Self and reach an awareness of the death of the Other. This is what lends an air of near resignation to *Adieux: A Farewell to Sartre*, published after Sartre's death and purposefully stark in style. "His death does separate us. My death will not bring us together again. That is how things are. It is in itself splendid that we were able to live our lives in harmony for so long," she writes at the end of the book.[23]

The writer uses this tone of noble serenity *after* the ordeal of his death. But the woman I knew was not so quick to resign herself, not so restrained or so calm. It is obvious that the Beaver's worsening alcoholism and nearly suicidal tendencies at the end of her life were caused by her inability to accept the idea of being permanently separated from Sartre, a possibility she had feared for such a long time.

Added to the pain Simone de Beauvoir felt regarding Sartre's blindness and decline was another conflict, which became worse and worse during the last six or seven years of Sartre's life. Sartre was surrounded by many loyal friends, including the entire staff of *Les temps modernes* and also many female friends. In addition, in 1965 he decided to adopt Arlette Elkaïm, who genuinely loved him and to whom he was very much attached.[24] Toward the end of his life, he hired as his secretary Pierre Victor (whose real name was Benny Lévy), one of the leaders of the Proletarian Left. In her biography of Sartre, Annie Cohen-Solal refers uneasily and cautiously to Sartre's "friendship with one of the leaders of the Proletarian Left, Pierre Victor. A Normalien and a philosopher, he [was] both his final secretary and his closest confidant. Their relationship was controversial and is difficult to analyze."[25] It was mainly the presence of these two people at Sartre's side that produced the drama in which the Beaver was a victim. Her coldness with Arlette turned gradually into outright hatred. As for Benny Lévy, at first she appreciated him as a quick and insistent conversationalist who made Sartre feel alive a little longer. But she soon realized that he tired Sartre out and attempted to use Sartre's fame for his own personal advancement. She tried in vain to get Sartre to extricate himself from Lévy's influence. The Beaver was irritated and saddened by the vitality of the two young people and by their growing animosity toward her. Simone de Beauvoir, Sartre's companion of fifty years, was both feared and scorned.

A detailed schedule involving several people had to be created for the sick and infirm Sartre. With some hesitation, the Beaver decided to spend all her afternoons by Sartre's side, reading to him. One day, when the time slots were first established, she told me as if searching for an excuse, "You see, I can't be with Sartre all day and night. I need to continue working, seeing my friends, living my own life. I spend my afternoons with him. Arlette, Benny Lévy, and other friends watch over him the rest of the time." Indeed, such an arrangement corresponded exactly to their entire existence. Did the Beaver voluntarily reduce her visiting time? Or did she do it because she was pushed aside by the others? I cannot say, for she spoke to me only briefly of her disputes with Sartre's entourage. Other people besides the Beaver, Arlette, and Lévy also came to see him. This kept him entertained but sometimes had serious consequences: at the old man's request some of them brought bottles of alcohol, which they hid in the nooks and crannies. This worsened the health of the famous invalid, and the Beaver had to hunt in all possible hiding places for the poison that was killing Sartre.

Relations gradually deteriorated between Arlette and the Beaver, primarily because of the many people who had become attached to the invalid but also quite possibly because of Benny Lévy.

The hostility grew as the months passed. The following is an example: In 1978 Arlette, Benny Lévy, and Sartre spent a few days in Jerusalem, where they had various contacts, both with Israelis and Palestinians. Upon their return, Benny Lévy drafted with Sartre the *Entretiens* (Conversations) on the problem of Palestine. These interviews were supposed to be published in *Le nouvel observateur*. Simone de Beauvoir found the text on Sartre's desk and judged it superficial and partial toward Palestine. Scandalized, she roused the gang of old friends from *Les temps modernes*. They had the same reaction to the text and managed to prevent it from being published. When he found out what had been done, Benny Lévy was furious. Simone de Beauvoir was extremely irritated when she told me about that incident.

Two years later, at the very end of his life, Sartre began a new series of *Entretiens* covering all his work, with the help of Benny Lévy. The project took them quite a while. That time, Lévy made sure Simone de Beauvoir did not have access to the tapes. And he delivered the text of the new *Entretiens* to Jean Daniel[26] in person, to be absolutely certain they would not be intercepted. When Jean Daniel hesitated upon discovering the contents, he received a personal phone call from Sartre, who enjoined him most firmly to publish them. *Le nouvel observateur* therefore published *L'espoir maintenant* (Hope now) in three installments in March 1980. This is not the place for a detailed analysis of these long texts. Instead, I suggest readers refer to the analysis given by Annie Cohen-Solal in her biography of Sartre.[27] Personally, I was shocked that Benny Lévy had clearly persuaded Sartre to go back on so many important points. It seems as though the old man were retreating inch by inch, forced back brutally by a sharp young man acting like a persecutor under Stalin. Quite obviously, Sartre no longer had the physical and mental strength to resist him. The interviews leave the reader with a feeling of uneasiness.

Simone de Beauvoir's resentment was commensurate with the transgressions Benny Lévy had committed. But what was even worse for her (and for him) was that for the first time she and Sartre were divided, at odds with each other: "On the other hand, since he was no longer himself, he was doing all this on Victor's [Levy's] instigation. . . . In those last discussions . . . Victor had pushed him to go against himself, to betray himself. . . . [Sartre] stiffened. . . . He was terribly torn by all this, he did not want to face the truth."[28] Arlette was also bullied by the young man. They would read the Torah together, for strangely enough Benny Lévy had switched from the Proletarian Left to militant Judaism. The Beaver was thus faced with two adversaries, one who enjoyed all the legal privileges of a daughter and another who had enough influence over the "little man" to counter her strength. I realized sadly that Simone de Beauvoir had planted the seeds of her own unhappiness: by never accepting marriage or wanting to raise a family, she had forced Sartre to adopt a daughter. From a legal standpoint, Simone de Beauvoir no longer meant a thing in Sartre's life.

Then the philosopher went to the hospital and never came back. He died April 15, 1980. In her stark manner, Simone de Beauvoir relates the last nightmarish days. What she does not say is that Arlette and Benny Lévy immediately locked up Sartre's apartment, even before his death, and prevented the Beaver from returning to get her things. Not long afterward, they moved all the contents of Sartre's home to a place unknown to her, without giving her even the smallest souvenir, the oldest pipe. As she described the incomprehensible fierceness of that act, it made me tremble to realize how much she was hated.[29] Sartre's death and the settlement of his affairs were fundamentally no different from what occurs daily in the bourgeoisie. It was pathetic and sad. The Beaver suffered their pettiness with apparent calm. Amazed, I asked, "Are you a fatalist, a stoic now?" She replied that what one cannot change, one is forced to accept. It seemed as though, now that Sartre was dead, everything else had lost its meaning for her. Death had probably upset the order of her values. I was soon to change my point of view.

A significant incident concerning the "threesome" occurred at the end of 1979 or the beginning of 1980. This incident showed me that the Beaver had lost none of her sharpness and aggression. In the last months of Sartre's life, in the midst of her problems with Arlette Elkaïm and Benny Lévy, the Beaver decided to publish a collection of letters Sartre had written her over his whole life, despite Arlette's objections. It was a way to finally mark the considerable importance she had had in the "little man's" life at a time when others were criticizing her and even attempting to supplant her. Why she chose to include letters written to other women is not clear to me. It seems strange to find these letters—although there are only a few—scattered throughout the collection of letters Sartre wrote the Beaver each time they were apart. My guess is that the Beaver wanted to give an idea of Sartre's various female attachments so she would not appear to be "the one and only," which she indeed never was. In her biography of Simone de Beauvoir, Deirdre Bair writes: "Beauvoir did ask Olga whether she could reprint the letters Sartre wrote to her, and Olga ordered her not to do it. Beauvoir told Olga to be prepared because she would print them anyway and to warn her sister Wanda that they both might be upset by some of what Sartre had to say about them. Olga was outraged. . . . Beauvoir blithely ignored her and published them."[30]

As for me, I knew nothing of the plans she was toying with. But one day the Beaver, ill at ease, made the following request: "There's something I want to ask you," she said. "Completely by chance I found a certain number of letters Sartre wrote you right before the war. I'd like to publish those letters along with the ones he sent me. Would that be okay?" I was all the more dumbfounded, having thought I had burned *all* of Sartre's letters in the Simonnets' furnace in 1942. I asked her where she had found that correspondence. She didn't know what to say. She stuttered that she had discovered them while cleaning. Later, when questioned by Deirdre Bair, she stated with irritation: "I did not steal them from his house: I just got them somehow. 'Toulouse' [Simone Jollivet],[31] for example—when she died, they were sent to my address and as [Sartre] was already blind I just never got around to giving them back to him. He gave Bianca's letters to me to read when he received them, and I just never gave them back. That's all. Nothing underhanded."[32] The Beaver was lying, all right, but she did not lie very well. She definitely had schemes, and her defense is illogical: it was not a question of letters from me to Sartre but from Sartre to me. Those letters should have been in *my* possession. I must have lent those letters to the Beaver to read, probably in autumn 1939, and the only explanation for this mystery is that she "forgot" to give them back and I forgot to ask for them. In other words, she had carefully put them aside and kept them for forty years, in order to bring them out again when she deemed appropriate. To her those letters were all the more precious because I told her that, in an iconoclastic fury, I had burned all the letters Sartre had sent me. In telling her this, I did not realize how that act of vengeance would affect her, steeped as she was in the value of the most minor thing written by the genius to whom she had devoted her life.[33] When I reflected on this later, I remembered a similar story involving André and Madeleine Gide: when Madeleine realized the kind of man she had married, she also burned all his correspondence. And André Gide never forgave her!

Still, I had to respond to Simone de Beauvoir's request. I

was anxious and hesitant. To escape that shocking situation, I asked to see those missives again. I went up to the Beaver's bedroom, sat down on her bed, and began reading them. I recognized Sartre's beautiful, delicate handwriting, but I had forgotten nearly everything contained in those love letters. Forty years had passed over that faded paper. Not only had I lost track of the sweet things he had written to me, but I had so vigorously suppressed that whole period of my life that I no longer recognized it. There were nineteen letters. The first dated from the beginning of July 1939, right after my operation, when I was still at the clinic. It began, "My dear little Polack, my love." The last is from September 14, 1939, several days after the war began and Sartre the soldier had left for the front.

I told the Beaver I needed a few days to think before deciding. I was very troubled. On the one hand, the mysterious reappearance of the epistles Sartre had sent me made me mistrustful and revealed the Beaver's hypocrisy. More than anything, I had the persistent feeling I should keep quiet about what had happened among the three of us. More generally, I believe that intimate relationships should be kept personal and not displayed for all to see. This goes to show how unacceptable I found the idea of publishing that correspondence.

On the other hand, I knew the Beaver was having a terrible time with a nearly blind Sartre on the verge of death. I could easily imagine how Sartre's courage was matched by the Beaver's pain.

These circumstances made it difficult for me to refuse to let her publish the letters from 1939, simply because she wanted to do so. I ended up giving her my consent with the express condition that she hide my name behind a pseudonym and eliminate any identifying evidence. She seemed relieved and deeply grateful. She explained that once she had finished her work she would return the originals, which were mine to keep. She said I could do whatever I wanted with them: save them, bequeath them to the Bibliothèque Nationale, or sell them at auction, possibilities I had never dreamed of. For a long time we spoke of it no more; out of discretion I never asked her how her work was progressing or what she had chosen as a pseudonym. Then, one day in 1983, she brought me printed copies of *Witness to My Life* and *Quiet Moments in a War*. The first thing I did once I got home was to look for "my" letters. I found thirteen of the nineteen I had just seen. My name had been replaced by "Louise Védrine." I was very confused and thought she must have given me such a French-sounding name to make it as different as possible from my own, so that no one would recognize me. But still, something was wrong. That name did not fit with "My dear little Polack, my love" in the first letter, a line the Beaver should have eliminated. Nor did it agree with the deep anxiety I felt as a Jew faced with the approach of the war, a feeling Sartre tried to alleviate. There was thus a discrepancy between my character and the pseudonym. Now that my impression of the Beaver has changed, I wish to add that, perhaps subconsciously, she wanted to eliminate my Jewishness, to erase it, because it caused her too many problems. But it would have been easy for her to find another Jewish-sounding name instead of Louise Védrine, which makes no sense at all.

I bitterly regretted not discussing this matter while there was still time. That absurd situation was partly my fault.

Why hadn't she asked me? Why didn't we decide *together* on that pseudonym? Now it was too late. The book had been printed. I decided not to blame her needlessly. I began to read the collection in its entirety. Shortly thereafter I stopped, completely disgusted by Sartre's way of pouring out his feelings, relating all his escapades in the most intimate detail as if addressing a slightly voyeuristic confessor; by the role the Beaver played as a mother, a sister in whom he confided, an indulgent or grumbling accomplice; by the immodesty of his confidences and his repeated declarations of love for the Beaver, by the litany of "My darling Beaver," and "I love you, my sweet little Beaver, I so want to see you again. . . . I send you passionate kisses." That jumble of sleeping around and clichéd expressions of love for the Beaver disgusted me.

I was so shocked that when I saw her again I blew up and told her that, had I known what the overall tone would be, I would not have allowed her to include my letters. Furthermore, I asked her, what could such a publication contribute to the fame of her companion? She blushed and plunged into an explanation I had already heard: a writer, she said, owes it to his audience to show himself as he is, even if what he shows is not to his advantage. I do not know where she got this idea of an artist. I find it monstrous, but it does show clearly the depth of her literary ambition: to show herself to everyone, to exhibit herself naked. Personally, I object to the lack of boundaries between private and public life. I do not believe a writer needs to divulge his bedroom or bathroom talk or show everyone his backside in order to be famous. To get back to the letters, I could accept that such was their relationship in private, but I could not accept without protest that it be made public. Their voyeurism had shades of exhibitionism and immodesty, with the aggravating fact that *she* was the one who decided to publish Sartre's letters, not he.

The book was out. I was powerless to change anything. Simone de Beauvoir had promised to return Sartre's letters but did not. Month after month for nearly three years, that is to say until her death in April 1986, she would arrive empty-handed at the various restaurants where we met. Sometimes I would ask, "Did you bring me Sartre's letters?" No, she had forgotten them again. After a while, I thought she would never return them. At our last lunch, which we decided to have in a restaurant on Avenue de Neuilly near my place, she was the one to exclaim upon arriving, "Oh! I prepared the envelope for you, but I left it on my desk again." That's a perfect example of what is known in psychoanalysis as a parapraxis, or misaction. Two weeks later, Simone de Beauvoir died.

Sylvie le Bon notified me by telephone. I attended the burial. I saw the Beaver's face again, a little swollen, stiffened by death. Her head was adorned with a beautiful turban. Her friends and family gathered sadly in the hospital room adjacent to the one in which her body lay. Then the procession set off. I was very tired and boarded a bus. Lanzmann, Sylvie le Bon, Jean Pouillon, and Bost walked arm in arm ahead of me, in front of the cars and the crowd. They moved along briskly, doing a sort of farandole. I thought they were trying to make themselves dizzy, to make Sylvie drunk with movement to ease her suffering. But there was, or at least there seemed to be, a sort of joy in the way they ran together. I thought to myself that they were perhaps relieved to be rid of their old friend, who had become too burdensome; their sorrow was perhaps mixed with relief.

I waited three months, then wrote to Sylvie to ask her to return Sartre's letters. She called me and set a time for us to meet at the Beaver's place. It was moving to be there in the absence of the woman who had lived every day in that magnificently large, bright studio. I explained to Sylvie that I had insisted on having Sartre's letters returned not because I was especially attached to them but because the Beaver had promised to return them after finishing her book but had not kept her word. At the time of Simone de Beauvoir's death, I still had faith in her uprightness and could not calmly conceive that she had failed to keep her word. I asked Sylvie if she knew what had caused the Beaver's resistance to returning those letters. "It's obvious!" she said. "She was afraid you would burn them." I was dumbfounded at such a flagrant psychological error. I did not allow those letters be published only to burn the originals later. That was absurd. And forty-three years had passed. My resentment toward Sartre had faded like a painting in the sun. It seemed obvious I would never have dreamed of destroying those relics of the past.

As I look back over the last years of my contact with Simone de Beauvoir, it seems that the tone of our relationship had changed, probably because the ordeals she had experienced caused her to view her life and our friendship differently. She sometimes questioned me straightforwardly, with more trust and spontaneity than before. For example, one day she asked, "Don't you like Sartre?" I replied that for me there were three Sartres: the first was a kind, generous, charming man; the second a famous philosopher and writer; as for the third, he was a boor, and he was the one I had known. To my surprise, Simone de Beauvoir thought a moment and uttered softly, "Yes, it's true that Sartre can be boorish sometimes." I wondered if she had recently suffered a particularly nasty bout of Sartre's boorishness. To better explain what I meant by boorishness, I told her for the first time and in full detail about my first physical relations with her companion. She said nothing.

Another day, she asked me a very personal question: "In all this time, why have you never written anything?" Apart from philosophical essays and some fifty pages I had added to *Peinture et temps*, I had indeed never been able to develop a single literary text. The few times I had tried to compose a story or autobiographical piece, my efforts had immediately failed. But that did not worry me too much, for I believed a person could live perfectly well without writing. I was respected as an excellent philosophy teacher, I spoke with the greatest ease, I truly loved my work and the contact with young people. A person could not speak and write well at the same time, I would say, half joking. I replied to the Beaver that I had once been mentally infirm and still considered myself as such. Struck by the expression I had used, she sighed, "We were so thoughtless, we were so thoughtless!" That was the alpha and omega of the forgiveness she asked from me. I had to settle for that.

I had not wanted to tell her the whole truth. Doing so would have meant adding that being close to two famous writers whose lives were dominated by writing and an ambition that squelched all other considerations, and suffering what I did because of them, I found the act of writing negative, even repulsive. If being a writer led a person to have such a lofty opinion of one's career, to hurt others and hold their feelings up to ridicule, then the simple fact that they were writers was enough to keep me from becoming one. Now that she is dead, I can express this harsh thought without the risk of hurting her.

In closing, I would like to try to explain the inner workings of the story of Simone de Beauvoir, Sartre, and me. I stress again our respective ages: when I met the Beaver she was twenty-nine years old and I was sixteen. I met Sartre the following year, when he was thirty-three and I was seventeen. This age gap undoubtedly had an important influence on our relationship, for in addition to their brilliant intelligence and culture, their age assured them an obvious superiority. They saw me as a little girl who needed to be trained and with whom they could toy. I saw them as mentors and models.

They could have been my parents. They were between two generations, dominating me enough to claim to guide me, to educate me, yet close enough to become my friends. Personally, I never dreamed of considering them pseudo-parents, but my analyst, Jacques Lacan, demonstrated that the unresolved conflict that tormented me was a result of their playing this role in my life, as though I had unconsciously pushed away my natural father and mother and replaced them with new, almost mythical parents. They had the prestige of intellectuals; they taught philosophy, aspired to become writers, already were writers. They had toppled the stereotypes that normally bridled sexuality and the morals that usually governed human relationships: all the elements were in place for me to fall into their trap. There was a hint of Nietzsche's immorality in their actions.

Only when Sartre slipped into my intimate relationship with Simone de Beauvoir did the drama begin. His arrival joined us in a triangle; as the third party, he was the clincher, so to speak. A twosome is a fragile structure that an intruder can slip into, but a triangle is a closed figure sufficient unto itself: nothing can break its geometric enclosure. I did not truly lose my head and imagine that this relationship would last forever until Sartre came along. I am convinced that, had I remained alone with the Beaver, my feelings toward her would have evolved naturally into a mild friendship. After all, there are many young women who fall in love with their teachers. It is a recurring theme in literature, a frequent occurrence in life.

What makes my case special, Lacan also explained, is that this figure was a reconstruction of the closed family unit, the classic triangle. I was caught in a rare psychological configuration: not only did I subconsciously desire carnal relations with my parents during my early childhood, as do all human beings, but in my case the desire was met in real life. I was in love with Sartre and transferred onto him the urges generally directed toward a father. Ordinarily, a child only dreams of this, but I had true sexual relations with him. That was a serious sin resulting from my strong identification with the Beaver: like all little girls, I identified with my "mother" (the Beaver) and sought to take her place as the object of my "father's" (Sartre's) affections.

The Beaver was vaguely aware of this, which explains her jealousy and strong objection to Sartre's permissiveness. My love for Mother-Beaver was also carnal, which is completely unusual and is a throwback to the very first years of childhood, to the primordial sensual attachment of a small child to its mother. That double emotional involvement marked me deeply and permanently. That is why I completely collapsed when the triangle fell apart. My emotional equilibrium wavered. It took me a lot of time, the help of a psychoanalyst, the love of Bernard and my children, and, I must say, a solid psychological base, for me to survive that fall.

This psychological analysis helps to explain why I was never able to put enough distance between myself and the Beaver; why, even though I had rebuilt my life around other things, I went back to her after the war. It also explains what always kept me from understanding her true feelings for me: I idealized her. That ideal image, created very early on, prevented me from grasping every facet of her personality and interpreting the signs of her hypocrisy. All of that explains my obvious naïveté: it resulted from the strength of this ideal and also from my strict notions regarding friendship and love. Not until her writings were published in 1990 was I finally hit with the harsh reality.

It was in reaction to the disgraceful contents of those letters, out of a sense of pride, of honor, that I decided to reply by telling my story as I had lived it. If those letters had not been published, I would never have dreamed of retelling or analyzing my past, much less publishing my story. My adventures as a young adult would have remained buried in my memory and then disappeared from all memory, and everything would have been well.

To finish my story, I will describe the day toward the end of Simone de Beauvoir's life when she asked me the ultimate question: "All in all, what do you think of our friendship, of our whole story?" After mulling things over for a moment, I answered, "It's true that you hurt me deeply, that I suffered greatly because of you, that my mental equilibrium was nearly destroyed, that my entire life was poisoned. But it's also true that without you I wouldn't have become what I am. Most importantly, you gave me philosophy. You also gave me a broader view of the world, a view I would probably never have adopted on my own. Consequently, right and wrong balance each other out."

I had spoken on the spur of the moment, from the heart. Simone de Beauvoir squeezed my hands, with tears in her eyes. Her heavy burden of remorse had been lightened.

Four years after her death, however, when I read *Letters to Sartre* and *Journal de guerre*, when, having decided to write my own version of events, I thought back to what I had said, I realized that my answer was enveloped in the fog that had always clouded my mind so that it could contain only a stunted version of reality. Simone de Beauvoir's death must also have freed me. From the grave she sent me that final message: the truth about her, about our former relationship, hit me square in the face. My eyes were finally opened. In the end, Sartre and Simone de Beauvoir did me only wrong.

Notes

Introduction

1. War diary (not translated). *Trans*.
2. Sylvie le Bon, Simone de Beauvoir's adopted daughter, holds the legal rights to de Beauvoir's works. It was she who had *Lettres à Sartre* and *Journal de guerre* published, probably according to de Beauvoir's wishes.
3. Louise Védrine is the pseudonym Simone de Beauvoir gave me in Jean-Paul Sartre's *Witness to My Life* and *Quiet Moments in a War*. Later I shall explain why.
4. Simone de Beauvoir was nicknamed "Beaver" by a classmate, as she describes in *Memoirs of a Dutiful Daughter*: "One day he [René Maheu] wrote in my exercise book, in large capital letters: BEAUVOIR = BEAVER. 'You are a beaver,' he said. 'Beavers like company and they have a constructive bent.'" In French, "beaver" is *le castor*, and the nickname "Castor" soon caught on. *Trans*.
5. Olga Kosakievicz, a former student of Simone de Beauvoir, formed the first "threesome" with de Beauvoir and Sartre in

Rouen. Olga was the basis for Ivich, a character in Sartre's *The Age of Reason*, and Xavière, in Simone de Beauvoir's *She Came to Stay*.
6. Deirdre Bair, *Simone de Beauvoir: A Biography* (New York: Summit Books, 1990).
7. In particular Gilbert Joseph's book *Une si douce occupation* [Such an easy occupation] (Paris: Albin Michel, 1991).
8. A series of lightweight novels in the collection Bibliothèque des chemins de fer, created in 1852 by Louis Hachette. *Trans.*

Chapter One

1. Originally *Esquisse d'une théorie des émotions* (Paris, 1939); English translation by Philip Mairet (London, 1962). *Trans.*
2. Albert Calmette (1863–1933) was a doctor and bacteriologist who helped develop the tuberculosis vaccine. *Trans.*
3. Zaza's story makes up a large part of Simone de Beauvoir's *Memoirs of a Dutiful Daughter*, trans. James Kirkup (New York: Harper & Row, 1959).
4. Zaza's death is described on page 360 of *Memoirs of a Dutiful Daughter*.
5. Sartre was in love with Dolorès Vanetti for many years. Either he went to see her in the United States, or she visited him in Paris. Dolorès "is the only woman who has frightened me," wrote Simone de Beauvoir in *Adieux: A Farewell to Sartre*, trans. Patrick O'Brian (New York: Pantheon Books, 1984), 305.
6. Simone de Beauvoir, *The Prime of Life*, trans. Peter Green (Cleveland: World, 1962), 26.
7. Ibid., 26–27. Such a promise logically lends itself to a certain voyeurism: whatever one person reveals about his or her lovemaking is provocative and exciting for the other (Deirdre Bair analyzes the voyeurism of de Beauvoir and Sartre). In addition, I believe that the promise to tell all intensifies feel-

ings and emotions: it is a game of mirrors—which often distort—in which two people take turns at being the passive "object," as in a game of catch. Feelings in such a relationship become infectious. The best illustration of this is how Simone de Beauvoir got Sartre to break up with me: she made him more and more disgusted with me.
8. Nelson Algren inspired the character of Lewis Brogan in Simone de Beauvoir's novel *The Mandarins*, trans. Leonard M. Friedman (Cleveland: World, 1956).
9. Olga later married Little Bost [Jacques-Laurent Bost, one of Sartre's pupils. *Ed.*]. That means they bred *two* couples. How ironic!
10. The French psychologist who introduced gestalt therapy to France in his work *La psychologie de la forme* (1937). *Trans.*
11. De Beauvoir, *The Prime of Life*, 169.
12. Originally *L'imaginaire: Psychologie phénoménologique de l'imagination* (Paris, 1940); English translation by Bernard Frechtman (New York, 1948). *Trans.*
13. In the United States at the same time this song was popularized by the Andrews Sisters; the words (meaning "I think you're beautiful") are Yiddish, not German. *Ed.*
14. Bair, *Simone de Beauvoir*, 214.
15. Jean-Paul Sartre, *Witness to My Life: The Letters of Jean-Paul Sartre to Simone de Beauvoir, 1926–1939*, ed. Simone de Beauvoir, trans. Lee Fahnestock and Norman MacAfee (New York: Scribners, 1992), 190.
16. Ibid., 223.
17. Jean-Paul Sartre, *The Age of Reason*, trans. Eric Sutton (London: Hamish Hamilton, 1947), 51.
18. Jean-Paul Sartre, *The Words*, trans. Bernard Frechtman (New York: Braziller, 1964), 104.
19. Henri Michaux, *Selected Writings: The Space Within*, trans. Richard Ellmann (New York: New Directions, 1945), 119.

20. Simone de Beauvoir, *Letters to Sartre*, trans. Quintin Hoare (London: Radius, 1991), 161.
21. Ibid., 29.
22. De Beauvoir, *Letters to Sartre*, 26. During that year, Simone de Beauvoir and Bost were lovers; Olga Kosakievicz was also enamored with Bost. Wanda was Sartre's official mistress. Sartre always spent several days each summer with his mother, whom he loved, and his stepfather, whom he detested, at Saint-Fargeau. Mrs. Morel ("the Lady") was a loyal friend of the two writers. Her very rich husband owned a gorgeous mansion and land in La Pouèze, near Angers, as well as a villa in Juan-les-Pins. She received her friends lavishly and with class.
23. Sartre, *Witness to My Life*, 190.
24. Ibid., 204.
25. Ibid.

Chapter Two

1. Sartre, *Witness to My Life*, 222–3. When Sartre was drafted in 1939, he was assigned meteorological work for the military. *Ed.*
2. Ibid., 225.
3. De Beauvoir, *The Prime of Life*, 283.
4. Sartre, *Witness to My Life*, 223–24.
5. Ibid., 226.
6. Jean-Pierre Azéma, *From Munich to the Liberation, 1938–1944*, trans. Janet Lloyd (Cambridge: Cambridge University Press, 1984), 4.
7. De Beauvoir, *The Prime of Life*, 317, and *Letters to Sartre*, 69–80.
8. De Beauvoir, *Letters to Sartre*, 156.
9. "The letter arrived after Bienenfeld's departure. . . . She didn't ask to see your letters, and I post-dated them—

verbally—which made perfect sense" (De Beauvoir, *Letters to Sartre*, 162).
10. Simone de Beauvoir, *Journal de guerre*, (Paris: Gallimard, 1990), 203.
11. De Beauvoir, *Letters to Sartre*, 159–60.
12. Ibid., 217. De Beauvoir of course used Bienenfeld's real name in her letters and diaries; the name was changed to Védrine in the published versions. A translation of the original French is used here. *Ed.*
13. Ibid., 226–27.
14. Ibid., 233.
15. Ibid., 273.
16. Ibid., 279.
17. Ibid., 281.
18. Ibid., 288.
19. De Beauvoir, *Journal de guerre*, 264.
20. Ibid., 192–93.
21. Bair, *Simone de Beauvoir*, 242.
22. Sartre, *The Age of Reason*, 54, 73.
23. Jean-Paul Sartre, *The Reprieve*, trans. Eric Sutton (New York: Knopf, 1947), 88.
24. Ibid., 92–94.
25. Ibid., 95–96.
26. Originally *Réflexions sur la question juive*; English translation by George J. Becker (New York, 1948). *Trans.*
27. The following is an excerpt from a series of interviews of Jean-Paul Sartre by Benny Lévy published in *Le nouvel observateur* beginning in March 1980:
Benny Lévy: When you wrote *Anti-Semite and Jew*, you thought that the Jew, if I may, was an invention of the anti-Semite. In any case, there were no such things as Jewish thought, Jewish history. Have your views changed?
Sartre: No. I retain that as a superficial description of the Jew

in a Christian world when, for example, he is caught up in the anti-Semitic thought that consumes him. I limited the existence of the Jew to only that. But I do know some Jews. At present I think there is a Jewish reality. The Jew believes he has a fate. I came to that conclusion because I was friends with some Jews after the Liberation.

B.L.: When you wrote *Anti-Semite and Jew*, did you gather documentation from many sources?

S.: No. I wrote *Anti-Semite* without any documentation, without ever having read a Jewish book.

These statements, these confessions, are utterly astounding. They reveal, among other things, the extraordinary thoughtlessness behind the theses of Sartre, who, after the massacre of a large portion of French Jews and foreign Jews living in France, sets out to write a brilliant book to show that the Jew exists only *relatively*, in the mind of the anti-Semite. What Sartre does is to permanently dissolve the Jews and forget what has occurred since time immemorial. This philosophical dissolution is a continuation of the Nazis' practice of physical destruction.

28. De Beauvoir, *The Prime of Life*, 348–49.
29. De Beauvoir, *Journal de guerre*, 304.
30. De Beauvoir, *The Prime of Life*, 354.
31. De Beauvoir, *Letters to Sartre*, 335, 336.
32. De Beauvoir, *The Prime of Life*, 366.
33. Ibid., 368.
34. De Beauvoir, *Letters to Sartre*, 342.
35. All the forms thus completed by the prefectorial administration employees were collected at Paris police headquarters, where the French and German authorities used them to make later arrests. It was an attempt to intimidate Parisian Jews, most of whom obeyed this "voluntary" declaration in

an effort to remain faithful to the (French) law. This is the file Mr. Klarsfeld claimed to have discovered hidden away in the Veterans Administration on November 12, 1991. His claim is open to debate. In January 1993 the file "affair" was far from being resolved.
36. De Beauvoir, *Letters to Sartre*, 348, 352, 360.
37. Annie Cohen-Solal, *Sartre: A Life*, ed. Norman MacAffee, trans. Anna Cancogni (New York: Pantheon Books, 1987), 159.
38. Georges Perec, *W, or The Memory of Childhood*, trans. David Bellos (Boston: Godine, 1988).
39. Together with Claude Simonnet, Simone Debout-Devouassoux, and Colette Duchâtel, I recently wrote a short history of Yvonne Picard, a member of the Communist Youth Movement. She was arrested on June 18, 1942, and deported to Birkenau-Auschwitz, where she died at the age of twenty-two. This history was published in May 1992 in the periodical *Esprit*.
40. Pierre-André Guastalla, *Journal* (Paris: Plon, 1951).
41. Member of the Resistance. *Trans.*
42. Paul Dreyfus, *Histoire de la résistance en Vercors* (Paris: Arthaud, 1975), 132. A very good overview of the battle of Vercors.
43. I have described some of the events and anecdotes included here from memory, using notes I took in a little diary I kept during the battle. I also used Paul Dreyfus's valuable book, as well as the eyewitness account given by Commander Pierre Tanant in *Vercors, haut lieu de France* (Grenoble: Arthaud, 1975).
44. Chambard, Claude, *The Maquis: A History of the French Resistance Movement*, trans. Elaine P. Halperin (Indianapolis: Bobbs-Merrill, 1976), 191–92.
45. Ibid., 189.

Chapter Three

1. Charlotte Delbo, *Mesure de nos jours* (Paris: Éditions de Minuit, 1971), 45.
2. David Rousset, *The Other Kingdom*, trans. Ramon Guthrie (New York: Reynal & Hitchcock, 1947), 168–69.
3. Perec, *W*, 157–58.
4. De Beauvoir, *Letters to Sartre*, 389–90.
5. Bair, *Simone de Beauvoir*, 598.
6. Note 11 of chapter 34 of Bair's biography states, "Bienenfeld (now divorced) had returned to Paris." The French edition does not contain this obvious error, probably for fear of legal action. Indeed, in 1990–91 I hired a lawyer in Paris to ask Éditions Fayard, which was having Bair's book translated, to eliminate any reference to my name and any explanation of the pseudonym "Louise Védrine." After causing quite a few problems, Bair agreed to substitute her own initials (D.B.) for my name.
7. Simone de Beauvoir, *She Came to Stay* (New York: Norton, 1990). Sartre's *The Age of Reason*, followed by *The Reprieve* and *Troubled Sleep* (New York: Vintage Books, 1973), constitute *Les chemins de la liberté*.
8. From Eugène Ionesco's first full-length play, entitled *Amédée, or How to Get Rid of It* (1954). Trans.
9. Simone de Beauvoir, *The Second Sex*, trans. H. M. Parshley (New York: Knopf, 1976), 471.
10. Ibid., 498.
11. Claude Lanzmann, a filmmaker, worked with Sartre on the review *Les temps modernes*. Trans.
12. Personal letter, which I have transcribed here word for word.
13. We were transferred to Paris in September 1954.
14. Guy Mollet was prime minister under President René Coty. Trans.

15. *Comité de vigilance universitaire pour la défense des libertés et la paix en Algérie. Trans.*
16. Simone de Beauvoir, *Force of Circumstance*, trans. Richard Howard (New York: Putnam, 1964), 336–47. These pages contain details on the Algerian war and describe Simone de Beauvoir's rage and indignation.
17. The "Appeal of the 121" for the right of young people to refuse to serve.
18. Of the publisher Éditions Gallimard. *Trans.*
19. Painting and time (not translated). *Trans.*
20. De Beauvoir, *Memoirs of a Dutiful Daughter*, 5.
21. Ibid., 6.
22. Simone de Beauvoir, *A Very Easy Death*, trans. Patrick O'Brian (New York: Putnam, 1966).
23. De Beauvoir, *Adieux: A Farewell to Sartre*, 127.
24. Cohen-Solal, *Sartre*, 452.
25. Ibid., 188. The last sentence is omitted from the English version. *Trans.*
26. Editor-in-chief of *Le nouvel observateur*. *Trans.*
27. Cohen-Solal, *Sartre*, 513–18.
28. Ibid., 515.
29. I am relating these events as described to me by Simone de Beauvoir. It is possible that, because of the extreme tension that developed between Benny Lévy and Arlette on the one hand and the Beaver on the other, the respective points of view on this serious dissention do not coincide.
30. Bair, *Simone de Beauvoir*, 598. Actually, besides the letters to Simone Jollivet, called Toulouse, and several letters to me, the collection includes only one long letter (sixteen pages) to Olga, describing Naples. Thus, either Bair invented the incident concerning the publication of Olga's letters, or more likely the Beaver gave up on publishing the letters to Olga and to her sister, Wanda.

31. The first of Sartre's letters in the collection is addressed to Toulouse. After many difficulties caused primarily by Arlette Elkaïm's reticence, Gallimard published the original French versions of *Witness to My Life* and *Quiet Moments in a War* in 1983.
32. Bair, *Simone de Beauvoir*, 598.
33. One day, perhaps in the 1960s, she confessed to me that she was convinced Sartre was a genius. She said that because of this she would no longer bother him by, for example, telling him to rest or stop taking Maxiton [a stimulant that supposedly increased intellectual abilities—*trans.*]. She had to let Sartre live as he pleased, whatever the cost to her.